SPIRITUALITY ON THE RUN

BALANCING OUR SPIRITUAL AND ACTIVE LIVES IN OUR CHAOTIC WORLD

Dr. Cecilia A. Ranger, S.N.J.M.

For paperback and Kindle

ISBN: 9781726670517

Printed in the United States of America

First edition

TABLE OF CONTENTS

Dr. Cecilia A. Ranger, SNJM

DEDICATION

I dedicate this book to the millions of talented, conscientious, hard-working women and men who spend long days in commitments visited upon them by family members, employers, friends, churches, civic groups, political parties, charities, and yes, even themselves.

With little time left for solitude, leisure, travel, time with family and friends, meditation, retreats, vacations, and dreams they have set aside for decades, they yearn for a sense of harmony in their lives. They seek to better balance the contemplative thoughtful parts of who they are with their talents for promoting the good of other human beings and the simple reality of earning a daily living.

Dr. Cecilia A. Ranger, SNJM

ACKNOWLEDGEMENTS

The greatest gift that a Spiritual Director/Guide or Retreat Facilitator receives, over and over again, is that of listening to life stories. For many decades I have heard one story repeated in many languages: "I am on overwhelm. I don't have time to meditate, get outside to breathe fresh air, laugh with my friends, go away for a retreat, even take a vacation. Seems I am running 24/7." Sometimes I am hearing the words of a Nike employee, other times a Protestant minister; then there are the sighs of the working mother, the teacher who stays up until midnight to correct papers, or the counselor who wonders what her own voice sounds like. Many, if not most of us, are busy with commitments 24/7.

Our fascinating but chaotic world offers us the enormous challenge of creating a rhythm in our lives, a life-enhancing harmony between action and contemplation. I recall a day, when I was a new math teacher of boys who came back from the service to finish their education; they were about my age, and one asked me one day after class, "Hey, Sister, whatcha doin' tonight"? That night I was in the Chapel praying, and realized that I had to figure out a way to balance my demanding active work schedule and my quiet time—or I would crack. It has been a lifelong chess game.

I wish to acknowledge those persons who met me along the way and invited me to "come apart and rest awhile," to learn to play a little better, to see God in all things and breathe a short prayer of gratitude. I also learned from them to capture un-committed moments: sitting at a traffic light, riding a train to see family, waiting in a doctor's office or an airport.

Some of those who helped me achieve what balance I have are:

- My mother, a playful extrovert, unofficial baby-sitter of the neighborhood, who taught all the kids how to make sling shots and stilts.

- My father, story-teller who never contradicted me but offered a story with his point of view, knowing I would get the point.

- Siblings and relatives, who ignored my perfectionism and did things their way without my advice.

- Friends, who invited me to play, travel, enjoy a glass of scotch, and argue theology, sometimes all night long.

- Retreat directors and counselors, both women and men, who chided me to enjoy my creative gifts as well as my organizational and get-things-done-efficiently ones.

- Students who are younger than I, who grew up in age when it was OK to go to a gym, to backpack across Europe, to sit for hours drinking wine with one's friends.

- The Holy Spirit, Spirit of Wisdom, Who continually knocked me off my goal-directed horse and made me ill so that I would experience a forced rest and reflection time.

- And books, wonderful books, writers who became my friends as I internalized their messages and taught their lessons to students. If one becomes what one reads, I am living proof that this is so.

PREFACE

This book was written for too-busy people. At one time in my life my schedule was so packed from 5:10 a.m. until 9:30 p.m. with teaching, extra-curriculars, supervising resident students, and cleaning floors of a large four-story Academy, that I had to rely on some thoughtful Samaritan to fill a plate with food for me three times a day, or I would not have had time to eat. And I, and also the superior in charge, interpreted this schedule as "holy obedience" because I was assigned to all the responsibilities which I was trying to balance. When I asked her what she preferred I do first, when I faced three duties scheduled for the same time, she threw up her hands and, walking out of the room, asked, "Who else can I ask"?

We may be president of a company, provost at a university, a single parent, or a farmer. We may have been commissioned to fulfill too many job responsibilities, and may have had others stacked on to these commitments by family, church, civic groups, friends, neighbors, school, and oh, so many other entities to which we "belong." We may be the super-conscientious types who feel it is our responsibility to undertake something, simply because we see it needs doing. Others of us have spent a lifetime trying (and failing) to learn to say "No" to everyone who has a request. Too many of us have been caught in the whirlwind of "to do's" and find ourselves squeezing out of our lives those things that cannot be counted at the end of the day, paid for in dollars and cents, documented on a timesheet, recorded on a performance review, or produced visible results. We think these things are expected of us—and often they are.

A convention of Church employees met in Los Angeles a few years ago, and I opted to attend a session called, "Living Above the Store." This referred to the practice, especially in Europe, of living above the family bakery or butcher shop, conscious of "work" and "responsibility" 24/7. The gentleman who facilitated the session asked, "What is the major cause of 'burnout' for dedicated Church personnel?" A plethora of answers filled the room: "Long hours. No breaks. Skipping vacations. Carrying the work load for colleagues who are supposed to be sharing." The variety of answers was telling, of course.

But, the facilitator then responded: "The major cause is Talent." He gave an example of an educator named Joe: Joe carried a full teaching load plus the coordination of several extra-curricular activities; he responded "Yes" to teach the math class for the colleague who had a dental appointment; he said "Yes" to the coach who asked him to supervise the basketball team after school because he had to prepare dinner for his sick mother; and his days became filled with a litany of "Yeses." Joe was talented; he could do almost anything well. And he was so organized that he figured out a way to fit all the extra "Yeses" into his schedule. By the time the facilitator finished Joe's story, he was facing an entire room of guilty, over-conscientious, laughing Church workers heading for their own species of "crash" or "burnout."

As one of the guilty worker bees present that day, as a woman religious who joined an apostolic congregation, as one who has always been given responsible positions, and as a person to whom spirituality is a very high value, I have made a practical life study of discovering ways to balance the pieces of a 24 hour day, to live the rhythm of an active and contemplative life.

In an era where people prefer other forms of gaining information, rather than reading books, it occurs to me that some personalities may wish to move on to getting the job done—not wasting time on "why" something might achieve results—but instead taking concrete steps to get where they wish to go. May I suggest that they read the latter more pragmatic part of each chapter.

In this book I have reflected on the diverse pieces of our lives—whether we serve as a corporate executive, a minister, a professor, a homemaker, a carpenter, a hair stylist, a safety engineer, or a plumber. I have peeked into places and times where we can find occasions for reflection, spirituality, and God, by whatever name we call our creator or supreme being.

Discovering that we can live a spiritual life on-the-run may keep us healthier, happier, and holier.

Dr. Cecilia A. Ranger, SNJM

CHAPTER 1:
SOUND BITE SPIRITUALITY
FOR THE SUPER STRESSED

Living a Centered Life in the Work Setting

"Maybe meditation is a good idea. But who has time for it?"

"Right. I've heard of studies about spiritual practices that relieve stress. But to me, that's just adding one more stress to my life."

"I know I need leisure for balance in my life, but...."

"Yup. I know. If I took time daily for centering prayer or meditation, I would probably need less sleep—at least according to folks who have time to write articles. But, I can hardly get in six hours of sleep as it is."

Sound bite meditations can take thirty seconds, consisting simply of a lifting of the mind and heart in gratitude to a Creator for the gift of Life.

So, what do we do about shaping a sensible, balanced interior life that facilitates our living a sane professional and personal life? Not many years ago we dreamed of the day computers and fax machines would cut our work weeks to 30 hours, make the use of paper an archaic phenomenon, allow us more time with our families, even make it possible to stand by the water cooler for five minutes to chat with a colleague as we waited for that fax response from the law firm. The dream popped like a helium balloon, leaving us with sixty to eighty-hour work weeks, huge bins of paper to shred, sleep-deprived states at least five days a week, and sound bite cell phone or text conversations with those whom we love—before we fall asleep on the sofa mid-sentence.

Yet we have the same human needs for solitude, reflection, inspiration, creativity, leisurely reading, quiet listening to music, and intimate relationships, as did the generations before us. And we have the same human gifts, one of which is the gift of time.

What then are ways some professionals find that what we do at "work" can empower us to respond to those needs in ways that leave us centered and sane? In my own living a super-stressed professional career, and in conversations with colleagues, friends, and students—especially those engaged in the corporate environment, but even those who work from their homes and those who are classified as "retired" or "house spouses"—I have discovered that some of these "sound bite" spiritual practices do contribute toward our living a more centered, serene, and even spiritual existence.

SOLITUDE

Rest Room hermitage. Few people will follow us to the rest room, even if their questions and needs are "urgent." I have spoken to mothers, harassed office personnel, and dignified administrators who are at the end of their tether with an employee or family member. Five minutes of escape to the rest room to breathe deeply, pray, or engage in positive self-talk can change the landscape and give us time to return to a state of peace and self-composure.

REFLECTION

Telephone ring as Buddhist meditation bell. Americans appear to be compulsive about answering the telephone on the first ring, allowing it to take precedence over every other engagement or commitment at that moment—even the person in front of us who has made a legitimate appointment to spend thirty to sixty minutes with us. Buddhists and also monks and nuns of Christian traditions ring a bell to call the community to prayer. We can consider the telephone as our meditation bell, letting it ring three times before we pick up the receiver, while we take three deep breaths and call to mind a centering word like "peace," "compassion," "balance."

INSPIRATION

<u>Website with inspirational saying for the week</u>. Whether we are eighteen or eighty, many of us sit down daily at the computer to do a spreadsheet, formulate a business letter or article, or write or Skype to our grandchildren. We can learn how to create our own web-site. Each week we can put an inspirational message or quote on the site and carry that thought through the day. A sticky note pasted to the monitor will do nicely until we can create a site. Others have found that a pack of 3 by 5 inch cards can be shuffled to provide a thought for the day, for oneself or for a gift to a friend or loved one. Some people carry a little pack of "angel cards" with words for meditation.

CREATIVITY

<u>Art center in corner of office</u>. A friend who had Alzheimer's—a former creative genius, I might add—dropped by my office daily, after her walk on our very lush campus. One day she would bring a leaf, another day an acorn, and sometimes a rock or flower. Each day I was able to re-create in my office a small "beauty corner" which delighted others, myself, and especially my friend who felt that she was contributing to the happiness of other people even though she was "losing it" intellectually.

LEISURELY READING

<u>Book or cards during coffee break</u>. We have called them "pocket books" for many years. Small inspirational books of poetry by Rumi or reflections by Joan Chittister do fit nicely in a purse, backpack, notebook, or even pocket. Many writers now offer a page a day, or short chapters that can be browsed

through during a coffee break, as we wait for a late client or business colleague, or rest during a lull in a meeting.

QUIET LISTENING TO MUSIC OR NATURE

Classical music or nature in background. Cities across the nation from Portland, Oregon, to Baltimore, Maryland, provide listener-supported all-classical radio programs. We can return to a sense of peace with this music as we prepare the details for a meeting, as we wait for a traffic light, or when heavy agendas keep us from falling asleep quietly at night.

Sometimes the tree outside the window offers us an opportunity to lift our eyes every hour to watch a bird on the magnolia branch or a squirrel in the maple tree. After staring at the computer screen for an hour, our eyes need a rest, and our spirit needs to smile at the wonders and humor of creation. It tickles us to watch the tireless squirrel jump from limb to limb or balance on the fence rail; we can also notice the nagging, clumsy crow telling the finches how they should fly.

Sometimes the Universe surprises us with its beauty: a double rainbow beams at us on the way home from work; or the Northern Lights take away the drudgery of "home work." We can take a few deep breaths, recall a happy memory, and thank the Creator for the gift of Life—our own and every being in the cosmos.

Intimate Relationships keep our hearts alive too. Lunch or break time with different colleagues to hear their unique stories unfold the mysteries of human life and give us an inkling of the interactions of persons with the sacred. Colleagues—as well as ourselves—often bring a sandwich or a left-over ready-for-the-microwave-oven. I have found that many employees enjoy a few moments of sharing stories in my office or in their space. Gathering with cohorts for a pizza and beer after work, stopping at a Thai restaurant at the end of a week-end marathon seminar to de-brief and process together the events of the last three days, and laughing over a short game of bridge at noon on Wednesdays foster relationships that can last for years.

We carry our needs of spirit, mind, emotions, and body to the work landscape as well as to our home and leisure settings. There is for each of us such a reality as "spirituality in the workplace" if we look at the opportunities in that venue for nourishing the desires that have been created into our very essence. Colleagues, as well as spiritual directors and mentors, will support us in our eagerness to find ever-new ways of living a centered, integrated, humane, spirit-filled existence in our stressful work climates.

Dr. Cecilia A. Ranger, SNJM

CHAPTER 2:
RE-CIRCUITING OUR MINDS
THROUGH LECTIO DIVINA

Re-Claiming an Ancient Practice to Bring
New Insights and Energy to Our Lives

MEANING OF *LECTIO DIVINA* (HOLY READING)

At break time, or awaiting a client, we can sometimes steal ten or fifteen minutes for reading. It has often been said that we become what we read. Perhaps it is even more true to say that we are shaped by the truths that we have not only read cursorily but also internalized and used as the foundation for our decision-making and our actions. In this sense our re-claiming *Lectio Divina* as a spiritual practice is a tool that will re-circuit our minds by allowing us to internalize the truths and values that attract and inspire us to positive action. These insights, now more deeply imbedded in our spirits as our own wisdom and value systems, energize us to speak and act as we wish—to do the good that we will to do instead of blindly going with the flow of what everyone else seems to be thinking and doing.

Lectio Divina is an ancient Christian practice which is being resurrected by persons from a variety of spiritual Traditions. In my courses on world religions I find that students are enthusiastic about using the method of *Lectio Divina* for personal and group reflection, using their own sacred canons or other inspirational literature as the basis for contemplation.

How do we describe *Lectio Divina*? And why is it attractive to people of every spiritual Tradition who wish to live an authentic, integrated life? Is there an uncomplicated pattern for carrying out this spiritual practice? Simply put, *Lectio Divina* is known as a slow, reflective, contemplative praying with the sacred scriptures of one's Tradition or sometimes with other inspirational literature. Benedictine monks and other Christians have been practicing *Lectio Divina* for about fifteen centuries, within the monasteries but also in the homes and villages and gardens of the world; for we can read a text and work with our hands while our spirits ruminate on the words that have touched our hearts.

What we call the Art of *Lectio Divina* begins with profound listening. St. Benedict referred to this kind of listening as "hearing with the ear of our hearts." The Hebrew Bible (1 Kgs 19:12) makes reference to the "still, small voice of God" and advises readers to precede committed action with the call, "Sh'ma Israel" (Hear, O Israel, in Dt 6:4). Christian Scriptures give the example of Jesus' retiring to the wilderness to pray (Mt 4, Mt 14, Lk 4), and often make reference to the ways Jesus recalls the Scriptures as an endorsement for action to uphold justice. In the Eastern Traditions Hinduism recommends thoughtful Yoga practices and Buddhism urges practitioners to live mindfully and to set aside moments for deep meditation. And our First World brothers and sisters remind us to be attentive and reverent toward all of creation.

PRACTICING *LECTIO DIVINA*

The process of *Lectio Divina* is indeed quite simple, and possible to adopt during short coffee or lunch breaks. Nevertheless, both Western and Eastern meditators who practice it have found that it leads to unforeseen transformations of their lives.

LISTENING WITH THE HEART

(LECTIO IS THE WORD THAT WAS USED BY BENEDICTINES.)

We begin *Lectio Divina* with "heart-hearing." Letting go of the noises outside and within ourselves, we let ourselves listen to the text in silence and in wonder. We seek to hear the intimate, personal message that the words and phrases speak to us. Since we are so accustomed to reading quickly the newspaper or e-mails or notices on the bulletin board as we enter the workplace, slowing down to muse on this message with our minds and hearts will be difficult at first. Our minds will want to rush in many directions to our "to-do" agendas, "should-have-done" lists, and all the people and noises and objects around us at the moment. However, even this first step, listening with the heart, is calming and centering for us.

MEDITATIVE INTERACTION WITH THE PERSONAL MESSAGE OF THE TEXT

(THIS STEP HAS BEEN CALLED MEDITATIO IN SPIRITUAL LITERATURE.)

Moving from attentive listening to meditating, we begin to interact with the words that have had a personal draw for us. We ponder the message of the words, allowing them to interact with our thoughts, our dreams, our hopes, our desires, our memories, our current understandings of life, and our standards of values. The Word of God, or the words of whatever sacred text we have chosen, touches and affects who we are at the deepest levels of our being. At this stage we begin to experience a deeper sense of integration: of our personal identity with our thoughts, our words, and our relationships toward others and toward all the aspects of our lives—even all other beings.

LOVING CONVERSATION WITH THE
SACRED VOICE BEHIND THE WORDS

(THIS PRAYER DIALOGUE HAS BEEN DESIGNATED AS ORATIO.)

We are moved to respond to the Source of the personal words that have touched our hearts and to the ways that this message interacts with the elements of our lives. In loving conversation, we dialogue about our responses with the Holy One, the Absolute, the Sacred Being who embraces us and invites us to become all that we can be. We find ourselves more and more able to expose our painful experiences, our failures to carry out our aspirations toward goodness, and our needs for healing or love or compassion or wisdom. It is this opening of the heart in loving conversation with the Sacred that disposes us to receive the grace and power to achieve our most precious and sought-after dreams.

REST IN THE PRESENCE OF THE ONE
WHO HAS INVITED US TO TRANSFORMATION.

(RESTING AND WAITING ARE CONTEMPLATIVE RESPONSES TO MYSTERY TRADITIONALLY IDENTIFIED AS CONTEMPLATIO)

The sacred words have invited us to transformation, we have internalized the personal message through meditation, we have opened our hearts to intimate dialogue and expressed a desire for transformation. Now it is time to rest, wait, enjoy the presence of the One who has offered such a gift to us. In tender and loving human relationships words are seldom necessary to heal pain, speak of love, demonstrate reverence, or ask for forgiveness. An attitude of wordless, quiet, loving reverence for the Mystery of the One who has invited us to a transforming embrace is expressed in contemplative silence, letting go, enjoying the presence of the Holy, allowing the Divine to act. We can let go of the over-conscientious attitude that everything depends on us alone; we often experience a sense of peace and assurance that "all will or can be well indeed" as Julian of Norwich assures her contemporaries.

Adapting *Lectio Divina* to Personal Style

In our decade, where we have dozens of choices for everything from housing to hemlines to toothpaste, seldom does "one size fits all" spirituality have relevance. *Lectio Divina* as a spiritual practice is attractive because it so versatile.

Texts we choose for reading can vary greatly. Commonly the sacred texts of the Tradition have been selected. We listen "with the ear of the heart" to the words or phrases that speak to the center of our being. Most often the text is a gentle invitation to us—not a sudden lightning bolt of insight or an intense sense of presence that leaves us ecstatic. However, some persons may select an inspirational poem or a colorful prose entry instead of canonical scriptures. Nature speaks to others, so the "book of nature" unfolds its wisdom for them. Surprises too, like rainbows or soft summer showers, delight the heart and lift the spirit.

At times the most salient "text" is our own past experiences. We move from one demand or responsibility to the other so quickly that we seldom have time to reflect on the meaning, lesson, or value of that experience. Nor do we take time to grieve losses before moving on. Selecting a passage from a journal or recalling a past encounter that puzzled us or delighted us is a marvelous option for all of us who live such a fast-paced existence. Any way that the Creator or the Universe speaks truth and goodness and wisdom can be *Lectio* for us.

Styles of meditation that we adopt can be learned from many spiritual traditions. Position and place are significant for many people. A comfortable sitting position with straight back and feet on the ground, or the lotus posture, facilitates the centering of the heart and mind. Shutting the office door may be the answer for some! In a silent place meditators can focus on breathing or they can speak interiorly or aloud a favorite word or phrase. Quiet centering exercises, in our regular "meditation corners," where we can sit comfortably and speak or chant a sacred word, serve as brief preparations for *Lectio Divina*.

We can then meditate on the words or images, allowing them to interact with our memories, dreams, concerns, regrets, joys, hopes, plans, relationships, the world that we cherish, and with all that we are and have at this moment. In this experience we are connecting our entire self to the invitation from the Sacred Source of our being. *Meditatio* empowers us to make ours the message we have heard, maybe for keeps.

Ways we converse with our Source of life are "tailored" to our personal styles and preferences. It matters little whether we use words, thoughts, or images to interact with the Holy One, or the Universe if one prefers that notion. I have known directees who write letters to God in their journals, musicians who compose song responses, poets who create verse dialogues, potters who have thrown a pot symbolizing their openness to do whatever is needed for the world. In the dialogue we can experience both the blessing and invitation of the Sacred One, who is ever-ready to offer us the transforming graces that we need, as well as the offering of our own memories, desires, appeals for forgiveness, or whatever we have discovered in our own hearts. The *Oratio* and *Meditatio* experiences of *Lectio Divina* sharpen our abilities to express who we are, to set boundaries, to be vulnerable, to be ready to act on our convictions, values, and commitments.

Savoring a sense of Presence can be both a challenge and a delight. Though few of us are skilled at "just being," each of us does have a human need to rest, to re-coup, to experience Sabbath at least once a week. Some persons take long walks, others play soft music, nature lovers watch a bee or gaze on a gladiola blossom. It is interesting that such quiet contemplation of Presence moves us out of ourselves and toward commitments to others and to care for our earth and all its glory and beauty and need for attention. Truly, the Divine Energy is with us in both activity and receptivity, but each of these realities has need of the other. We are able to do nothing for a while, to be present to the Mystery of God, to return briefly to the words of invitation if that is necessary.

We will discover that this rhythm of contemplation and action that follows the *Lectio Divina* practice gradually carries us along a helix, an ascending spiral of personal transformation. We cannot disconnect *Contemplatio* from commitment.

EXTENDING *LECTIO DIVINA* TO A GROUP

I have visited Latin-American base Christian communities, where books are often rare, and I was deeply stirred by those who gathered to share the ways that they had carried out during the week the message of a common biblical passage that all of the members had previously read and agreed upon for personal reflection. This kind of *Lectio Divina* meditation on a selected text can also serve as a springboard for group spiritual direction or group spiritual transformation, or group commitment to a ministry or mission.

Many people are looking for a group with whom they may share their experiences, insights, and values in a climate of trust. Group *Lectio Divina* can be a means of sharing community, growing in self-confidence, fostering committed relationships, discovering meaning in our life projects, and consecrating our work and ministries to God.

It is important to recognize that contemplation is not a goal which we achieve through a spiritual technique. In actuality contemplation and action are two faces of the same love.

Action (Greek *praktikos,* Latin *operatio*) and contemplation (Latin *contemplatio*) are the two poles of our spiritual lives. Our lives are a dance, a rhythm in which we oscillate between committed spiritual action and receptivity. Moving toward the activity pole, we find ourselves actively cooperating with the grace and energy of the Divine to reach out to the needs of other persons in our world and to all of those ways that human beings are responsible for "keeping the earth." But we need the transformative love acquired through contemplation to continue to extend this kind of energy without burning out. That is, we contemplate the Divine Being just as that One is (*theologia,* contemplation of god) and we contemplate the Divine in all of creation (*theoria physike*, contemplation of god in the many).

As we look back at the transformations we have experienced in our lives, we recognize that the rhythm, the oscillation back and forth, has become a helix, an ascending spiral. We watch ourselves change, through *Lectio Divina*, and we recognize this ascending spiritual phenomenon: while we serve more generously in a broader arena, we have also drawn closer to the Source and Center of all being. As time goes on we discover different ways of experiencing the presence of the Divine and we notice that we ourselves are energized to respond to more and more needs in our environment, the structures that shape our churches or nations, and the individual persons whom we encounter at work and at home, and even in our travels and leisure activities. We find that we have re-claimed an ancient practice, re-circuited our minds, and through so doing, have brought new insights and renewed energy to our lives.

Chapter 3:
Meditation Attachments for a Computerized Lifestyle

Creating User-Friendly Software

We may need to admit that some of us sit at our computers up to 14 hours a day, especially if we must meet a deadline on a project, or a book or dissertation. Though we read that it is a good idea to take a short walk every hour, few of us have established healthy patterns for respecting our bodies or our spirits as we drive our selves toward these finishing lines.

My computer talks a "bong" when I turn it on and offers a familiar electronic "hum" to let me know it is alive and well. It even flashes "winks" at me to let me know that it is ready for action wherever I wish to send the mouse to animate the cursor. But our computers have some user-friendly talents that can do more than work for us eight to sixteen hours a day. They can actually play-pray, lifting our spirits to transcendence as well as relaxing our tensions with touches of humor.

We can draw down a short message under our by-line, as much to lift our hearts for the day as to let others in on our special concern at this moment of our lives. These spiritual invitations can be sticky-taped to the computer or kept on file to be highlighted and lifted up with different seasons or circumstances.

Some categories that may touch our spirits, deepen our reflections on life, make us richer personalities, provide us with substantive conversation material, broaden our experiences of culture and religions, and genuinely enrich our lives are the following. At one time I collected quotes in a notebook, as many writers do, for easy access. I also listened for possible quotes as I sat in airports or bus terminals when I did more travel than I do at present. To "jump start" the process for us, the following sections will offer a few examples, and some readily available sources.

INSPIRATIONAL QUOTES

The fact that I can plant a seed and it becomes a flower, share a bit of knowledge and it becomes another's, smile at someone and receive a smile in return, are to me continual spiritual exercises. Leo Buscaglia

POLITICAL GEMS

We need to reject any politics that targets people because of race or religion. This isn't a matter of political correctness. It's a matter of understanding what makes us strong. The world respects us not just for our arsenal; it respects us for our diversity and our openness and the way we respect every faith. Barack Obama

SHORT POEMS

One by Shawnee Kellie

One word can spark a moment,
One flower can wake the dream;
One tree can start a forest,
One bird can herald Spring.

One smile can bring a friendship,
One handclasp can lift a soul;
One star can guide a ship at sea,
One cheer can obtain a goal.

One vote can change a Nation,
One sunbeam can lift a room;
One candle wipes out darkness,

One laugh will conquer gloom.
One look can change two lives;
One kiss can make love bloom.

One step must start each journey,
One word must start each prayer;
One hope can raise our spirits,
One touch can show you care.

One voice can speak with wisdom,
One heart can know what's true;
One life can make a difference,
One life is me and you....

LITTLE LEGENDS.

An old Cherokee is teaching his grandson about life.

"A fight is going on inside me," he said to the boy. "It is a terrible fight and it is between two wolves.

One is evil – he is anger, envy, sorrow, regret, greed, arrogance, self-pity, guilt, resentment, inferiority, lies, false pride, superiority, and ego."

He continued, "The other is good—he is joy, peace, love, hope, serenity, humility, kindness, benevolence, empathy, generosity, truth, compassion, and faith. The same fight is going on inside you—and inside every other person, too."

The grandson thought about it for a minute and then asked his grandfather, "Which wolf will win?"

The old Cherokee simply replied, "The one you feed."

SHORT, SHORT BIOGRAPHIES.

Barbara Bush — the only woman besides Abigail Adams to be both a wife and a mother to a president of the United States — was born in New York City on June 8, 1925. In 1945 she married George H.W. Bush, who became vice president in 1981 and president in 1989, the same year she started the Barbara Bush Foundation for Family Literacy. In 2001 her son George

W. Bush was inaugurated president. The former first lady passed away at her home in Houston, Texas, on April 17, 2018.

PEOPLE POWER.

The power in people is stronger than people in power. Saji Ijiyemi

KIDS' WISDOM.

When I asked my son (5 years old) how his day was, he said it was awesome. I asked him what made it so awesome — his response was "because I wanted it to be." Tanya Niedzwiek

ANIMAL QUOTES.

The animals of the world exist for their own reasons. They were not made for humans any more than black people were made for whites, or women for men. Alice Walker

ONE-LINE JOKES.

A clear conscience is usually the sign of a bad memory.

HEBREW BIBLE QUOTES.

It is within your close reach to follow the Torah in speech, feeling, and deed. *Deuteronomy 30:14*

CHRISTIAN BIBLE QUOTES.

Now we see things imperfectly, like puzzling reflections in a mirror, but then we will see everything with perfect clarity. All that I know now is partial and incomplete, but then I will know everything completely, just as God now knows me completely. *1 Corinthians 13:12 (NLT)*

QUOTES FROM THE QUR'AN.

Do they not see the birds controlled in the atmosphere of the sky? None holds them up except Allah. Indeed, in that are signs for a people who believe. *Quran (16:79)*

QUOTES FROM THE VEDAS.

The one who loves all intensely begins perceiving in all living beings a part of himself. He becomes a lover of all, a part and parcel of the Universal Joy. He flows with the stream of happiness and is enriched by each soul. *Yajur Veda*

When we are deeply moved or saddened by an experience, or when we are overwhelmed by events in life, we simply "cannot find the words to express how I feel." We can then call on the words of others in families, circles of friends, cultural history, Spiritual Traditions, or the great body of literature written by thoughtful human persons throughout the centuries. An inspirational thought written by a person who has lived through what we are experiencing will lead us to realize that we are never alone but we are one being of a human family that has lived for many centuries.

Dr. Cecilia A. Ranger, SNJM

CHAPTER 4:
CALMING THE CHAOS

Contemplation is the
Heart of Every Engagement

"Meditation has gone mainstream." Even for us "workaholics." That is the title of a program I tuned in to a few days ago. After many centuries of spiritual practice by Jews, Christians, Hindus, Buddhists, and other Spiritual Traditions, moderns of the twenty-first century have re-discovered this ancient wisdom: contemplation (a Western term) and meditation (an Eastern term) do calm the chaos inside us. As a result, we are empowered to do the tasks we must do in our active lives with a heart that is more peaceful and ordered and thus the person is energized to reach out to the most exhausting of tasks.

Mahatma Gandhi, who was trying to drive a colonial power out of his homeland and keep Hindus and Muslims from slaughtering one another, said, "I have so much to accomplish today that I must meditate for two hours instead of one." Gandhi coupled his fidelity to contemplation with his nonviolent resistance campaign. In the end, he achieved many of his political goals for his people. Simply meditating on Gandhi's quotes stirs me to a new zeal for engagement in our world and its hurts, but also a renewed conviction that the rhythm of contemplation and action make this commitment possible.

Within the last decade studies of ADHD in children, teens, and adults have uncovered some very important information about the workings of our brains during both activity and silent meditation. One of my graduate students became interested in studying brain activity during a phase of hyper-activity and also a time of respite for children diagnosed with attention deficit hyperactivity disorder. Her findings were similar to those mentioned by Lidia Zylowska, MD, in *The Mindfulness Prescription for Adult ADHD*. That is, neuro-imaging studies of those engaging in mindfulness practice seem to influence the brain regions affected in ADHD, pre-frontal cortex and anterior cingulate cortex. These brain regions are critical for self-regulation: control of attention, thinking, and emotions. James Monroe, "The Adolescent Brain on Meditation," citing Sara Lazar and her team at Harvard Medical School, says that meditation enhances the areas of the brain associated with well-being, self-regulation, and learning—and decreases the volume of the amygdala, which is responsible for fear, anxiety, and stress.

These studies are quite fascinating, and I mention them here only because they are having practical application in our schools and some institutions of healing, such as prisons. Some schools are providing for short silent meditation periods morning and afternoon, for example. And Vipassana meditation has been used in prisons in India for about 25 years and is offered voluntarily to prisoners and staff members in other countries as well.

Vipassana means to see things as they really are, and this form is one of India's most ancient techniques of meditation. It was taught in India more than 2500 years ago as a remedy for universal ills; in short, it helped people with the Art of Living. For almost two decades the technique of Vipassana has been quite successful in reducing the rate of recidivism within prison populations where it has been employed on a regular basis. Information can be found in studies like *Vipassana Meditation Rehabilitation and Research Trust for North American Correctional Facilities* in the United States.

Understandably few of us are eager to adopt Gandhi's practice of meditating for one or two hours before major presentations. And few of us will go away for a 10-day

Vipassana retreat. Nevertheless, many very busy people are finding 10-20 minute "coffee-break" periods to sit in quiet and solitude, in morning and afternoon; some companies have begun to provide small meditation rooms for their employees.

So, what might a short meditation period look like? We can find helpful articles that describe 23 different types of meditation, one of which may suit our style of being, places where we live and work, and the times we are able to set aside. I have taught the "Five P's" to make it do-able for people. I imagine any mnemonic device to facilitate one's moving quickly into a meditative mode will do. Here is a sample:

PLACE

A corner that is quiet, perhaps a little dark or softly lit, separated from usual activities seems to be agreeable to most persons. However, it is possible to meditate as one travels Amtrak between Baltimore and Washington D.C. or from Portland to Olympia. One woman told me that she curtained off a corner at the edge of the living room, using her grandmother's old sewing machine as an "altar" and placing on it a few objects that were sacred to her. Whenever she could not find her husband—or a child—she peeked around the corner and there he was. The need seems to be universal; my sister found her young son Thaddeus sitting in a dark closet, and he responded to her "Why?" with "I was jes' thinkin'." And, busy mothers have been known to lock the bathroom door for ten minutes.

POSTURE

Those who are in great physical shape find a Yoga posture effective. Others use a straight-backed chair, feet on the floor, hands cupped or resting on the knees. Some seek a church or chapel, sitting on an hard-backed bench or kneeling on a kneeler. I recall doing this at age six, in fact, when churches were left unlocked. Energy seems to flow better if it can circulate smoothly through the body.

PRESENCE

Eyes either partly open, looking down, or closed, one gathers oneself, aware that one is in this place at this time, wholly present to the self and often to the Holy One, God, Jesus, Buddha, Muhammad, or a Wisdom figure.

POINT

We can point and center ourselves by focusing on the breath, a mantra, a word, a lit candle. Some suggest that we breathe in through the nose and breathe out through the mouth in a regular rhythm, attending only to that activity. We can repeat a word (love, integrity, peace, Jesus), or a mantra or line from Sacred Scripture ("I have loved you with an everlasting love") as we do so. Others discover that finding a focus point by gazing on an object, like a statue or lighted candle, serves as a focus point that holds their attention.

PURPOSE

Though our purpose is to engage in quiet meditation or contemplation, we find that we need to renew that purpose often during every session. I have read that the human mind is so active that we can concentrate only seven seconds. To return from the many diversions like "What am I going to cook for dinner?" or "Why did he say that?" we simply return to our point of focus: breathing, or the word we have chosen, for example. Yes, over and over again.

When people tell me they (or I) cannot find any words to pray or even quietly meditate for a few minutes, these words of Mahatma Gandhi inspire me: "In prayer it is better to have a heart without words than words without a heart."

CHAPTER 5:
USING SPIRITUAL PRACTICES TO EMPOWER THE ADVOCATE, TRANSFORM PUBLIC INTEREST LAW, AND TRANSFORM COMMUNITIES

Maintaining one's integrity while also fulfilling the demands of a profession or a calling finds us struggling with inner conflicts at times. In the long run, we know that we want to hold on to our integrity; we have to go to bed each night caring about ourselves, and we want to be right with our God when we end each day.

Would you believe that two lawyers are Guiding Lights for my daily spiritual journey? The first was a sophisticated Englishman, Sir Thomas More—who became lawyer, Ambassador, and Lord Chancellor in England—but finally was beheaded because he refused to take an oath which would perjure himself. The second was a little lawyer from India— Mahatma Gandhi—who believed, also with the price of his own life, that a non-violent approach to conflict would bring more peace, unity, and justice to his nation than would the use of weapons.

Both Thomas More and Mahatma Gandhi came from families who had means. Both were men of integrity and self-discipline. Both embraced spiritual beliefs and practices that steadied them interiorly—in the midst of political and religious resistance and social chaos.

Who these men were as persons became one with their Vocation to act in the world which offered to them daily frustrations and challenges. Parker Palmer says that a vocation does not come from a voice "out there" calling me to become something I'm not—but a voice "in here" calling me to be the person I was born to be.

Mahatma Gandhi used to advise his followers to meditate for longer periods of time when pressures were great and their workloads were staggering. Robert Bold, in *Man for All Seasons,* wrote of Thomas More:

> (he was) a man with an adamantine sense of his own self. He knew where he began and left off . . . But at length he was asked to retreat from that final area where he located his Self. And there this supple, humorous, unassuming, and sophisticated person set like metal, was overtaken by an absolutely primitive rigor, and could no more be budged than a cliff.

Their sense of Self, their personal self-discipline, the energy from their spiritual practices flowed out from these two men to the large community of human persons, with a rich gratuity, even in the face of Resistance. The starting point lay within the Center of the Self. As Bede Griffiths says: "There are three ways to the Center. You can have a near-death experience. You can fall desperately in love. Or you can begin the practice of meditation. Of the three, meditation is probably the most reliable starting point."

Other writers have attested that this energy from within the Self spills over to enliven new energies for persons and systems. Cynthia Bourgeault explains: "The solitary work of prayer is ultimately communal, and in a powerful though mysterious way it upholds and maintains the life of this planet at an energetic level." She adds:

> If we really wish to change the planet, to become a sign of hope in a broken world, all we really need to do . . . is to narrow the gap between means and ends: between the gospel we profess and the gospel we live out, moment to moment, in the quality of our aliveness. . .I believe that spiritual practice is good

for the global community; we cannot keep positive life forces to ourselves; we are driven to share them with the people who need us most. . . Spiritual practices like meditation lead us to realize with the speculative science of quantum physics, that we are encountering interdependence at energetic levels.

As lawyers, counselors, spiritual directors, parents, corporate decision-makers, doctors, and professionals in all human enterprises, we make better-informed, wiser decisions if we are deeply reflective persons. We may not discern as quickly—and some decisions do demand immediate responses—but we do not have to re-visit these questions and solutions to problems as often if we consider them on a deep level at the outset.

So, practically, what are some rather simple spiritual practices that give us the discipline to stay calm in the midst of external pressures?

- Daily centering prayer, focusing on a word: energy, oneness, gratuity, sacred, Jesus, Allah, Adonai

- Meditation, attentive presence to one's breathing, energy of one's body, a beautiful rhododendron, or spiritual insight during many moments of the day

- Mindfulness in all we do, recalling Divine Presence when crossing thresholds, lifting up a short reflection when phone rings, walking to the bathroom, peeling potatoes

- Daily consciousness examination, review of each day, identifying energy-enriching experiences and also energy-zapping ones

When we can let go of anger, hurt, remorse, every day before retiring, we find that we need less sleep. We don't react adversely to surprises. We operate from the Center of the Self. We learn to know our own goodness, wisdom, and beauty—gifts we can give freely to others, without depriving ourselves. Those conflicts between our integrity and demands of others that do not sit well with us are easier to resolve.

When we accept the deepest Self—and the Self energized by the Divine energy—this positive energy catalyzes clients or colleagues to give their best life-enhancing gifts—not their meanness and smallness. And, bit-by-bit we make inroads toward social justice in seemingly immovable people and also organizations. These two lawyers, Mahatma Gandhi and Thomas More, give us a Light to follow: from the discipline of daily spiritual practice, to a richer sense of self, to a desire to serve others more graciously and gratuitously, and to invest energies into changing systems so they begin to recognize the rights of every human being.

We become, each day, more and more connected with the person we were meant to be.

CHAPTER 6:
HOLY HOUSEKEEPING, MINDFUL MOVING

Living Tranquilly in a Messy Universe

I imagine that many of us, of all ages, have become list-makers. We may even have followed the suggestion to create the list and prioritize it at the end of the day, so we can sleep better and "hit the ground running" the next day. Often we do not include breathing time in those lists, though we yearn for some tranquil moments amidst all the "to do's."

Few can argue that our world is not incredibly complex: a world of acceleration, value conflicts, tenuous employment, religious pluralism, strained relationships, fear of terrorism—still, many persons have a deep desire to touch those things that are lasting, meaningful, and even Sacred. Laity, members of religious communities, and ministers of Western and Eastern Traditions seek Spiritual Directors or Guides or Companions to assist them with focusing, centering, looking at their gifts, knowing their True Self, and relating to their loved ones, colleagues at work, people whom they serve, and the Divine or Holy One whom they believe is present to it all. The Spiritual Director can make it possible for the seeker to take the first step toward that journey to the center of the self and that presence to the Sacred: the way of simple attentiveness to every object and happening. Living mindfully. Re-collecting ourselves often during each day.

For centuries Christians have spoken and written about "recollection" and Buddhists about "mindfulness" to describe a human experience that precedes conceptualization or categorization or expression in symbolic words, actions, rituals, or art forms. Living in a "recollected" or "mindful" way keeps us aware and allows us to see the happenings of life with a greater clarity. It keeps us centered, present, and tranquil as we move through the realities that we meet each day. Awareness can even augment short and long-term memory, for we attend to something long enough to eventually recognize, name, categorize, and send it on to our long-term memory bank.

Here I use the word "mindfulness" instead of "re-collection" for this pre-symbolic state of awareness. It is the activity that eventually gives rise to insight, words and other symbols. I call this stage the "attending" that precedes our recognizing and focusing on the object or reality; in a short time, we human beings will objectify it, categorize or segregate it, and symbolize it with a name. The prior unfocused awareness is a deep knowing, much like the experience of holding the one whom we love on the horizon of our consciousness. *Vipassana* (insight) meditation and Christian contemplation facilitate our prolonging this kind of attentiveness. All of us are offered moments of "re-collecting" and re-centering ourselves—Holy housekeeping—as we move through the activities of twenty-four hours of each day.

Words like "mindfulness," "re-collection", "awareness," "attending," or "being" cannot be described in a "How To" manual. But we can perhaps identify with some of the following descriptions of the experience of mindful or "attend-full" living. Note that these examples are **not add-ons** to an already long list of commitments; instead they are ways of attending to each task on that list so that we marry contemplation and action. They are:

NON-JUDGMENTAL OBSERVATION

Our minds observe without criticism or judgment or condemnation. We allow things to be exactly as they are, without making any decisions about our responses. We do not reject any unpleasant states that seem to arise within us— irritation, agitation, frustration, fear, depression—nor do we reject the existence of whatever reality is before us. We just observe.

PARTICIPATORY OBSERVATION

Mindfulness is a wakeful experience of living. We are alert, observing, and participating. We are aware of emotions and physical sensations, though this experience of observing is not an intellectual awareness. We observe both the phenomena within ourselves and the reality before us.

NON-CONCEPTUAL OBSERVATION

At this stage we are attentive but we are not yet involved with thinking or formulating concepts. We are not involved with ideas relating to what we observe, opinions about the reality we are attending to, nor are we relating it to memories of encounters we have had in the past. We register that which we observe, but we make no comparisons or analyses. The experience of mindfulness precedes perception, thinking, evaluation, and decision.

PRESENT-TIME AWARENESS

Hence, mindfulness happens now and in this setting. If we remember what happened before, that is engagement of memory. If we say, "Oh, yes, this means such and such...," we are moving to thought or conceptualization. If we are comparing this observation with another, we are analyzing.

IMPARTIAL ATTENTION

We are watchful, taking in both the "good" and the "bad" without clinging to or avoiding either. In short, we do not suppress or repress our own responses, nor do we shut out whatever confronts us.

NON-EGOISTIC AWARENESS

Though we are participatory observers, we do not relate the here and now experience to ourselves. We do not refer everything of which we are aware to "me," "mine," "my," "our," "we," "us." We notice a sensation, of pain or joy or sadness, but we do not say, "I am sad." We do not emphasize, add to, subtract from the experience before us, we simply let it "be," avoiding every inclination toward narcissism.

NON-GOAL-ORIENTED ATTENTION

Living mindfully means that we do not push for results, as we so often do in our lives—especially when we make our daily to-do lists or look at the aspects of life pragmatically. We do not try to see the usefulness of that of which we are aware; nor do we try to accomplish anything with it. We let go of achievement or goal-orientation in relation to that to which we are attending.

MIRROR-LIKE REFLECTION

We reflect only what is happening in the present, without bias. We note what is taking place, exactly as it is transpiring. It is as if we reflect what we see in a mirror, not through any filters of our own design.

AWARENESS OF IMPERMANENCE OF ALL LIFE

Because life continues to flow and change, we watch the cycles of life: birth, growth, maturity, death. We observe all of nature and the passing phenomena that each reality displays itself at this moment. We watch the universe outside of us, and the universe within—each changing, developing, becoming. We live in freedom, unattached to the changing phenomena of life. We do not "hang on" for fear of losing what we have.

I have observed that younger list-makers and older persons fearful of moving toward Alzheimer's disease, speak often of their "poor memories." Awareness achieved through "mindful living" or "re-collection" or "carefully attending-to" or "holy housekeeping" can even augment short and long-term memory, for we attend to something long enough for it to move to our long-term memory bank—to eventually recognize, name, categorize, and retain it.

As I indicated in a paragraph above, Christians have been speaking about recollection for centuries and Buddhists have sought to live mindfully for a long period of time. Those who embrace various religions of the world seek such a human experience that precedes conceptualization or categorization or expression in symbolic words, actions, or art forms. Living in a "recollected" or "mindful" way does keep us living in the present but also keenly aware of the changing phenomena in our rapidly changing world. But, while we are keenly aware of each happening, we can remain centered and tranquil even in the midst of chaos.

This is not the end of the story. Christian contemplation and Buddhist meditation school us to observe with care, to be aware of every created reality just as it is. To accept ourselves, others, our world, the Universe, and Life. In *Vipassana* (insight) meditation we attend reverently to one item at a time; when the mind wanders and we lose focus, we return to a Sacred word or the process of breathing in order to re-center ourselves. In Christian acquired contemplation, the process of re-focusing is similar. Living mindfully—attending to the phenomena of our outer universe as well as our inner world—disposes us for meditation or contemplation, a mental habit that carries over into all of our life activities. We become more centered, peace-making, responsive to others' needs, world-serving, non-violent citizens of this ever-changing and somewhat messy planet. That is a great description for "spirituality on the run."

Dr. Cecilia A. Ranger, SNJM

CHAPTER 7:
RECLAIMING THE COMMONS

A Fresh Look at Earth Space

My nephew works for large companies who wish to be environmentally sensitive in both the production of their goods and services and the treatment of by-products. Many if not most of us have been proud of the ecological advancements the U.S.A. has made during the last forty years. Nevertheless, recent forest fires, major hurricanes, tsunamis, tornadoes, heat spells, floods, and other disasters have destroyed homes and businesses, as well as snuffed out the lives of many persons of all ages—reminding us that the issues of Global Warming and environmental destruction do not seem to be going away! That is why I want to implore us once again to "Reclaim the Commons" in our personal and work lives.

A short time ago I was asked to present a spiritual perspective on sustainability of our resources, specifically that of our water resources. Though I serve as a theologian and as a spiritual director, I was asked to speak to the group of business persons, environmentalists, water engineers, and representatives of other groups because I was one of the members of the steering committee for the Northwest Bishops, in preparing their fairly recent pastoral letter on the Columbia River and its watersheds.

I touched briefly on three points which I wish to share in this chapter: (1) the purpose and hope of the Bishops, (2) the spiritual principles undergirding the letter, and (3) some practical suggestions for implementation of the challenges of the letter to all of us, no matter how busy or sophisticated we are.

First, the Bishops, with Bishop William Skylstad as Chair, chose this stewardship of water topic as one that is a universal concern: to Jews, Christians, Muslims, Buddhists, persons of all spiritual traditions; atheists and agnostics; scientists and farmers; people of every nation and culture. Water, not gold, may be the resource over which future generations will wage wars! My SNJM congregation has taken water as one of their mission priorities: Water as a Human Right and a Social Responsibility.

Before we wrote, we listened! The steering committee heard representatives of many groups give readings of the Signs of the Times in Portland, Seattle, Hanford, Toppenish, Umatilla, Castlegar BC, Spokane, and Hermiston. We held listening sessions with those engaged in agriculture, fishing, aluminum manufacturing, provision of power—in Spokane, Yakima, Astoria, Beaverton, Helena, Clarkston, and Pablo (Montana). We consulted experts in many fields, from water equality to engineering to theology. Personal concerns for livelihood were very real, and very passionate! Some people still warned us to "separate religion and science." As one man put it, "Why don't you bishops and members of the steering committee go back to doing spiritual things, and stay away from environmental issues"? Those of you who had the opportunity to read the pastoral letter noted that the opening page quotes Bishops and Pope John Paul II on the urgency of environmental education and of balancing the ecosystems—for the future of the earth, others, and even oneself. The recent publication, *Laudato Si,* by Pope Frances refers to our Mother Earth as our Common Home.

It was the hope of the Northwest Bishops, and many of us, that interfaith groups, scientific groups, people in many sectors of society, would talk together, strategize together, and act together to make water a sustainable resource. That implied negotiation and give-and-take of all parties. To that end, booklets, outlines, videos, and other resources were made available for persons of all ages.

Second, many people in the Northwest tell me that they do not belong to any organized religious body–but that spiritual values are primary in their lives. The pastoral letter, calling us to stewardship of our water resources in the Northwest, rests on a number of spiritual principles. The sub-heading is: "Caring for Creation and the Common Good." In the pastoral letter we spoke of a "sacramental commons." At one time, people grazed their animals on a "commons," a town square that belonged to everyone in the village. Now our "town squares" are shopping centers! It was quite exciting to me to read the words on the cover of a *Yes!* magazine, "Reclaiming the Commons."

Plato used a Ladder of Beauty motif in his dialogues for the Symposium, moving up the ladder from the Beautiful Forms of Earth to the Ideal of Beauty. In a sense, the Bishops' pastoral letter lets us stand on seven rungs of a ladder of beauty as we reach toward the ideal of sustainability of water resources where we live and work.

THE IMMANENCE OF THE DIVINE AND THE GOODNESS OF CREATION

Two spiritual themes that emerged included the *immanence of the Holy in creation* and the *goodness of creation,* both of which result from the Creator's blessing and presence. All creation is pronounced "good" by the Creator in the Book of Genesis. Therefore, water and other sustainable resources have an inherent value given to them by the Creator—other than that of providing goods and resources for humanity.

At least four principles of an environmental ethic might speak to each of us:

1. Do no harm to other creatures except as it is necessary to meet basic human needs.

2. Do not alter the Earth except as it is necessary to meet real human needs.

3. Recognize relationships among human beings, all life and the Earth as a whole.

4. Care for the Earth and for living creatures, recognizing that all creatures, human and nonhuman, are members of a community of life and of mutually life-giving ecosystems.

We need an environmental ethic akin to the Hippocratic Oath, "Do no significant harm to the waters," adding to conservation a responsibility for restoration too, insofar as this is now feasible.

A SACRAMENTAL UNIVERSE AND A SACRAMENTAL COMMONS

The concept of a sacramental universe and a sacramental commons reminds us that every being reflects the beauty of Divine presence and creativity. This letter localized these notions for the watershed region. The philosopher Plato believed that human beings knew beauty before their souls came down to earth to live with bodies. Spiritually, since grace means "free gift" we could say that from the beginning a Creator was lovingly seeking in *freedom* to bestow himself/herself on all beings. Consequently, nature is never actually purely and simply secular; nature is graciously endowed with the touch of the Creator.

HUMANITY'S ROLE IN CREATION AND RELATION TO THE REST OF CREATION

Human beings have a reflective consciousness; we understand that we have *responsibilities* to Creator and to creation. But, we also possess the intellectual ability to *manipulate* the laws of the physical universe. Some respondents have expressed their appreciation that the document has moved away from past approaches that advocated human *domination* over creation, in favor of stewardship. Some people have also objected to the word "stewardship" as having overtones of hierarchical domination, with humans rather than God being at the top of the pyramid. However, it was our hope that we will come to see ourselves as the *consciousness* of creation, and as the caretakers of those parts of creation entrusted by the Creator to us.

The Relationship of Environmental Caretaking and Economic Justice.

Environmental concerns and economic justice are closely related. Much environmental despoliation benefits a minority of affluent people(s) and harms the poor, especially the ethnic poor. In contrast, all people should share in a just distribution of the goods of creation. We have traditionally called this distributive justice, in ethical terms. One thing I have learned in my life is this: just because something is possible does not make it ethical.

A Prophetic and Challenging Pastoral

The challenging times in which we live call for a *prophetic* pastoral letter, as several bishops have suggested. The prophets of old read the signs of their times and offered sometimes strongly worded statements, calling their people to acknowledge the errors of their ways and to convert to a new way of living. The pastoral letter could be a strong statement of the ecological problems faced by people in the watershed region and throughout the world, and a call to conversion to attitudes and actions of respect and appreciation for all of creation.

Church Modeling of Sacrifices for The Common Good

The pastoral letter calls upon people to make sacrifices for the **common good**. This is often a distasteful stance, in an individualistic America. In fact, when I use those two words, people wonder what in the world I mean. In response to an environmental pastoral letter, institutional commitments to reduce environmental harms can have a strong impact. So can personal commitments. In our region, for example, where people and the waters they depend on have suffered from chemicals used for gold mining, agriculture, gasoline production, nuclear energy, lawn maintenance, fracking for methane, and other purposes, environmental stewardship for the common good will be a challenge to all people to reverse these consequences.

Pope Francis' research on our Common Home, as well as his pastoral attention to every living thing that dwells here, expands the Northwest Bishops' letter to include the entire world, extending even to the entire cosmos. *Laudato Si'* has extended our care and concerns for what I am calling "earth space" to the entire universe.

A Sense of Place in a Regional Pastoral Letter

This environmental pastoral letter is uniquely bioregional and international. It will be most enduring and effective if it demonstrates both a sense of place and a consciousness of environmental issues and principles that transcend a particular geography and are important in all geographic areas. In a region that is only 10% "churched," the pastoral could be a means of drawing people together to consider spiritual perspectives on ecological issues. A strong sense of place, of the particularity of this watershed, paradoxically would awaken in people of this and other places a sense of the universality of environmental issues, an awareness of universal principles proposed for addressing them, and insights into the spiritual dimension of the world in which we all live—and hope, with our children, to thrive.

The steering committee divided this Pastoral Letter into several sections: The Rivers of Our Moment, The Rivers of Our Memory, The Rivers of Our Vision, and the Rivers of Our Responsibility. In a number of places, we distributed one page from a reflection sheet on the River of Our Responsibility. It suggested both community projects and personal actions for sustainability.

Talking together in groups like these, planning together, and acting together so that we can **Reclaim the Commons** for human communities—and all ecosystems—will make our efforts more comprehensive, sustainable, and FUN. And, we will leave earth space, and all beings that walk on the soil of Mother Earth, a beautiful home for our posterity!

I view many young people and millennials as deeply spiritual people, though they are not necessarily church-goers. They commit hours of their time to preserve our sacramental commons, our common home: cutting brush, cleaning rivers, picking up refuse on shorelines, and assisting with community gardens. They ride their bicycles so we can breathe purer air, eat vegetarian food so we can use land to raise food for hungry children, buy second hand or vintage clothing so they can spend their money on helping the homeless who wander our streets and sleep under our bridges. We of every age can do likewise.

Truly Earth Space is our space in the Universe, and our lived spirituality embraces and protects all of its beauty as the heritage we wish to pass on for another 13.5 billion years.

I want to add that our simply acknowledging, as we drive to work, the beauty of the red leaves; being delighted at the deer that eats our rosebuds; experiencing awe at the child's questioning—all are, in a sense, prayers of thanksgiving to the Creator of Our Common Home.

Dr. Cecilia A. Ranger, SNJM

CHAPTER 8:
TODAY'S DARK NIGHT EXPERIENCES:

Spiritual Crises
That Help Make Us More Beautiful

When we are loaded with commitments coming from every direction, we sometimes become just plain weary, tired of feeling burdened, not motivated to engage with anybody or anything. We feel depressed, spiritually depleted. We may be reasonably hopeful that we will learn new skills, possibly become more loving and generous persons—even personally stretched in every way. Nevertheless, we want some clarity and balance: is this just plain overload and depression, or is it a spiritual challenge that can reap some positive benefits?

When I was very young I read what was to me a very refreshing and enlightening book about what was then a contemporary view of dark night experiences, the focus of which was predominantly psychological. His now classic spiritual book is called *Life Within,* and the author was Dominic Hoffman O.P.

Way back in the 16th century John of the Cross gave us a classical description of the agonies and ecstasies of this experience in the poetry of his classic *Dark Night.* The first verse of the poem is translated:

In an obscure night
Fevered with love's anxiety
(O hapless, happy plight!)
I went, none seeing me
Forth from my house, where all things quiet be.

I struggle to describe to ministry students, and spiritual directors engaged in *practica,* some clues to identify our own dark nights, descriptions for contrasting the manifestations of this spiritual crisis with those of psychological depression, and ways to open ourselves to spiritual maturing because the Divine who allows us to receive the gift of dark night experiences has actually honored us. For it is true that spiritual emergencies, as Christina and Stanislav Groff name them, are often confused with psychological illness. At times the person receives medication to get rid of the symptoms, without being assisted in a search process to discover if this may be a spiritual experience that is an invitation to something personally rich indeed. I do not say that we by-pass medical intervention, and often the use of medication to alleviate suffering and to stabilize the person is both indicated and imperative. But I have witnessed persons who seem to be over-medicated for their emotional and psychological pain, and I see little evidence that their spiritual sufferings are also being addressed by an experienced spiritual director or guide or counselor.

At the outset, let me admit that every adverse or painful occurrence is not necessarily a dark night experience from a Loving God. Gerald May, in *Care of Mind, Care of Spirit (109-110)* offers some clear distinctions that can serve as a basis for initial questioning to achieve clarity about whether the sufferer is enduring the pain of depression or moving through a spiritual dark night toward growth. The examples he suggests do touch interior and personal experiences as well as their outer manifestations; these can be illuminating to both the sufferer and the spiritual director or mentor or counselor who is journeying with the person.

So how might we profile a dark night experience for contemporaries? I borrow from May's writings to describe some specific manifestations that a person may be walking with God through a contemporary dark night or some kind of experience that is at least spiritually confusing, challenging, and painful:

- People experiencing what we call a dark night are mystified that they are still effective at work and are still able to help others.

- People struggling with an interior dark night and often a feeling of God's absence in their lives still retain a sense of gentle-not-bitter humor.

- Those undergoing a dark night experience remain compassionate toward others, not self-absorbed (as is often the case with clinical depression).

- Whereas, in primary depression one feels wronged and eager to be rid of the feelings, the one undergoing a dark night feels there must be a rightness about this experience and that he will probably grow from it, not wishing it to be otherwise.

- Though help and understanding may be sought, there is for the person undergoing a dark night no urgency to "get me out of this." (There is hope at the end of the tunnel, in other words.)

- Other people do not feel annoyed or distanced by the person suffering a dark night experience. (One mother told me that her three children kept their distance when she was undergoing a period of depression, but that they actually sought her out when she was going through a spiritual dark night.)

- It would be arrogant of me to presume that I can anticipate every occasion where persons may encounter purifying dark nights. A Loving Creator will "tailor" every spiritual invitation to transformation to the gifts and burdens and personal style of the individual. Nevertheless, it is safe to say that our spiritual life is expressed in every dimension of our lives. So, the fallout of spiritual dark nights can carry over to all of these aspects of life. The person who desires spiritual integration, and a balance between her many engagements and her interior life, may wish to take a look at some of the "pieces" of her life to try to discern how they fit together to form a composite picture of who she is. A spiritual director, close friend, or faith sharing group may help us during this process, perhaps at a retreat. Some aspects of our lives which we may choose to consider are:

PHYSICAL HEALTH
- Medical assessment
- Health habits: sleep, diet, exercise

EMOTIONAL HEALTH
- Evaluations of and by other people
- Attitudes toward life in general

LEISURE, LIFE-GIVING ACTIVITIES
- Restorative engagements
- Life-enhancing experiences

DRUDGERY ACTIVITIES
- Dealing with 'Shoulds' and 'Musts'
- Successful Struggles with that which bogs one down

SOUL NOURISHMENT
- Finding what makes the spirit soar
- Knowing when one is happiest
- Discovering when one is most oneself

RELATIONSHIPS
- Affirming
- Challenging
- Freeing

PROFESSION
- Satisfactions
- Challenges

INTELLECTUAL UNDERSTANDINGS
- God
- Self
- Others
- World and place in world

PERSONAL PRAYER
- Style
- Regularity

COMMUNAL PRAYER
- Satisfying components
- Preferences

SPIRITUAL DISCIPLINES
- Mind-fasting attitudes and other healthy spiritual notions
- Discipline with regard to use of material resources

SPIRITUAL PRACTICES
- Commitment to service of others
- Regular meditation
- Use of beads or other prayer aids
- Tithing

This may seem like "overwhelm-plus" but investment of a weekend in such a spiritual assessment may be worth it, especially if we find ourselves feeling miserable at work, edgy with our family, alienated from our friends, and just plain mad at the world. Life does offer us both burdens and dark nights as well as successes and ecstatic moments. Both can contribute toward wholeness.

Dr. Cecilia A. Ranger, SNJM

CHAPTER 9:
DUTY FREE MOMENTS FOR THE TRAVELER

Rest the Lap Top or Tablet or iPhone

In my professional life I have traveled via airplane, train, tour bus, double-decker hop-on-hop-off bus, cruise ship, commuter boat, automobile, and some wild taxis. I have observed people grab for the cell phone even before they make it through the security line; and, on the other end of the journey, the cell phones are whipped out as soon as it is announced that we may do so. Other travelers begin to take out their laptops before they are fully ensconced in their seats near the departure gate. Body posture and movement are also indications of restlessness; the foot is tapping or moving up and down nervously, and eyes are cast often at the watch. In airports, bus depots, train stations, and ferry dockings food and beverages keep us occupied. We seem to have an insatiable need to keep our hands and all members of our bodies busy every moment and during every interlude, connected to those we just left or to those whom we will soon meet, engaged as fully as possible with the world around us during every waking moment. Do these behaviors affirm for ourselves that we are fully alive?

What if we "stole" moments for stillness between our activities and engagements? What if we simply allowed ourselves to be quiet and reflective until we heard a call to board the airplane? How can we enrich the time during our wait for a train, a bus, a taxi, a commuter boat, or a traveling companion?

I call these times "duty free." What could travelers "do" while we fly, drive, tour, taxi, or cruise toward a designated location? If we now must show up at the airport two or three hours before our scheduled flights, how can we "spend" the interludes of waiting? Since I often needed to be interiorly focused, externally organized, at least somewhat relaxed in front of an audience, and ready upon arrival to make a presentation or participate in a meeting, the captured intervals between numerous commitments helped me center myself emotionally, collect my thoughts—and avoid developing ulcers, to boot.

The two hours at the airport before we are called to board a carrier are "grace" (gift) time. Colleagues and family members accept our absence, so we can meet the two-hour norm as a national and international safety requirement. We are stuck. But we are also gifted and blessed with time to spend as we wish. So, what if we:

— Carried a small Rumi (or other) poetry book to pull out of our computer cases and read reflectively, *Lectio Divina* style, pondering the relevance and application to us of words that jump out of the text with a personal message for us and which often come to us as an invitation to re-examine our values and goals?

— Used beads as tools for spiritually centering and re-focusing, as do many Catholics, Anglicans, Muslims, Hindus, and Buddhists, often discovering that repeating rhythmically mantras or prayers on these beads triggers in us an awareness of the need for transformation of our person and of our service to humankind?

— Consciously offered a prayer to God or an energy-wish to the Universe for each specific person seated in our section of the airport, desiring that anything that weighs heavily on each heart will be lifted at least for that day?

Though the driving time during a five-hour highway stint to make a presentation does not leave our eyes or hands free for reading or fingering beads, nevertheless we can relish in other ways five precious hours of freedom from work. Some that I have found revitalizing are:

- Chanting an original psalm of praise for everything beautiful that comes to my consciousness as I drive along the highway: oak and fir and fruit trees, a herd of llamas, a flock of geese, an orange sky at sunset, or a double rainbow.

- "Writing" gentle thoughts for a journal or a letter into a tape recorder at my side, or formulating pleasant or affirming words that "I should have said" and "Plan to say" but "Forget to say" to colleagues or loved ones during an ordinary rushed day.

- Listening to tapes, DVDs that feed my soul and inspire me to act justly and sensitively to persons of every culture and religion and later to participate with scientists, theologians, environmentalists and others who value our responsibility for "keeping the earth."

The extended tour bus ride to Las Vegas for a meeting can be a "close encounter" with the Mystery of the Sacred, or the mystery of the human being at my side. Though I have learned to sleep on buses, trains, and planes, so I can be ready for action and not suffering from jet lag when I arrive on location, I have also found it refreshing to simply listen to Mystery. Life offers us many revelations as we listen with our hearts and minds and spirits as well as our ears. What about listening mindfully to:

- The mystery of pain in the heart-broken woman who tells me that she is going to visit her two sons, both of whom are in prison; the worried mother who shares with me that her son was injured in Iraq and has been sent to Germany for treatment; or the crestfallen older man who admits that he feels lost and lonely since his wife died?

- The Mystery of the Sacred touch present in every non-human being that exists in the variable terrains we traverse along the way: craggy mountain, desert of rolling sagebrush, alert doe with her baby deer, flashes of lightning or driving rain, and the wonder of a newborn filly feeding at mother's breast?

- The mystery of the great conundrums that human beings face daily: why religious people kill each other in the name of God the Creator of all beings, why we cannot share the resources of the world so that all persons have enough to eat and shelter over their heads, why technology and finances and precious oil cannot be used for the common good of humankind, why we continue to suffer from racism and sexism and ageism if all human beings have been created equal and are priceless simply because they exist?

The wild taxi ride to make it to the hotel on time for the conference after a late-arriving flight can ignite our desires to replace order with chaos and a great appreciation for what is life-enhancing over capitulation to defeat. We are comfortable with familiar venues and with our proven abilities to take the routes that get us where we are going in a timely manner, However, being shaken out of our comfort zone can lead us to break through walls and open boxes of our creativity, if we are willing to see possibilities in the highly unlikely circumstances that crash into our lives. Though we could be so frightened that the following possibilities sound contrived, taxi rides can offer us opportunities to:

- Consider all the accomplishments we would like to achieve during our lifetimes. Spiritual writers offer us the unwelcome suggestion that we should once a month contemplate ourselves on our deathbeds. Maybe the natural risks, challenges, and dangers we encounter daily offer us invitations to dream of a meaningful future for ourselves, and our loved ones.

- Sharpen our awareness of the people who live on the streets and sleep on sidewalks and manhole covers, re-motivating ourselves to ask congresspersons to shift resources in their direction, align ourselves with coalitions to provide food banks and housing units for the underprivileged, or contribute to those organizations that enable people to maintain their dignity by providing opportunities where they can help themselves.

- Ask our Higher Power that we may learn more about trusting people to carry out their work or their tasks in life their own way, even though it would not be the way we would choose to do so. Though this takes a lot of letting go, the result is often far richer than we could have anticipated.

The long day on the cruise ship with a business associate or aging family member offers us a respite from professional engagements. However, some of us regard such a five-day cruise as another commitment. We take computer, cell phone, professional journals, and brief case—on the off chance that we will have some free time from entertaining, dining, or taking the land excursions that are part of the package. Though it is difficult to relax and "just be" or "do nothing," cruise time can be spiritually productive if we:

- Watch the ways the colors on the waves make myriad patterns throughout the day, patterns that we can capture on film and have mounted in our offices, affording us throughout the year daily excuses to return to that experience of wonder and rejuvenation.

- Note the sea of contrasts among the symbols of culture that we encounter and the diversity of personalities from all age groups and nationalities, stretching our pre-conceived ideas about other societies, enriching us with new symbols of art and meaning, re-examining our values and our goals in life, and questioning whether we need to rush from one change to another without grieving our losses.

- Give our senses a re-birth, by re-awakening ourselves to the objects that are meant to gladden each sense: the beauties of sunrises and sunsets that our eyes pass over without seeing as we drive to work, the glorious sounds of lapping waves that our ears would usually ignore as background noise, the salty air that fills our lungs with a healing inhalation and restorative cleansing to replace the smoggy air that we draw in through shallow breaths, and the tasty meat sauces that delight the palate that seldom savors and dines instead of simply eating to keep alive.

In our professional lives we may do a lot of travel via airplane, train, tour bus, double-decker hop-on-hop-off bus, cruise ship, commuter boat, automobile, or taxi. These could provide duty free times for us: away from cell phones, laptop computers, even free from eating junk food or chain-drinking lattés to keep us alert and moving. We can "steal" moments for stillness between our activities and engagements, allowing ourselves to be quiet, reflective, personally enriched during these interludes, and even more focused, at ease, and purposeful toward the commitments that await us.

CHAPTER 10:
THE INFINITE AND THE OBVIOUS

We Seek the Infinite and
Walk the Paths of the Obvious

Saint Augustine prays to God, "Our hearts are restless until they rest in Thee." We are searchers by nature, continually reaching out for the "More." We enjoy blazing new trails. We make scientific discoveries. We seek ways to improve our business enterprises. We fly all over the world to create new markets. As soon as we can speak, we ask questions. We feel we never love others adequately, nor do others love us as deeply as we would desire. Our minds and our hearts seek The Infinite, which we might call the ultimate, or some, the Absolute. And those who excel in an Olympic sport will tell us that they continually press their bodies toward new limits, new "infinites." Even our physical beings seek that which is ever beyond us. We seek The Infinite with our entire beings.

Yes, our hearts are ever restless, attempting to move beyond the present realities of our lives, striving to reach what is, in a sense, the unreachable. And yet, Spiritual Traditions claim that the Sacred—Trinity, deepest Self, the Absolute—also lies in our very beings. Spiritual Traditions also look beyond us and explain in various ways that the Divine Presence is to be found in every reality: animal, plant, mountain, ocean, sun, moon, cloud.

Traditions explain God's Presence in the universe in at least two ways. We all them Pantheism or Panentheism.

The essence of Pantheism is a profound reverence for Nature and the wider Universe and awed recognition of their power, beauty and mystery. Some Pantheists use the word "God" to describe these feelings, but the majority prefer not to, so as to avoid ambiguity. From this feeling flows the desire to make the most of our present life in our bodies on this earth, to care for nature, and to respect the rights of humans and animals in general. We choose to focus on the vibrant and urgent here and now, rather than on invisible realms, spirits, deities or afterlives. We believe that mind and body are an inseparable unity, and so we do not expect personal survival after death. Instead we look forward to a natural persistence of our time on earth, in the actions and creations we leave behind, memories people hold of us, and recycling of our elements in Nature. Pantheists consider that "God" is identical with Nature and the wider Universe, and use the term (if at all) primarily to express their own feelings towards Nature. (*from World Pantheism, 2016*)

Many sensitive and spiritual people described to me their love of nature, the exhilaration they feel when they ski down a mountain, or their recognition of something really mysterious and meaningful about these special moments of their lives. They do have a taste of Something beyond themselves. In short, the pantheist looks at a Redwood lovingly and sees the Divine Presence.

Unlike Pantheism, which holds that the divine and the universe are identical, Panentheism maintains an ontological distinction between the divine and the non-divine and the significance of both. In Panentheism, God is viewed as the soul of the universe, the universal spirit present everywhere, which at the same time "transcends" all things created. Panentheists hold that God is present in and throughout nature and humans, but also transcends them and is much greater than they are. Basically, Panentheism is a form of belief in a creator God, while Pantheism is not. The Panentheist would look at the same Redwood and praise the creative wisdom and power of the God who created the Redwood and all things living. Panentheism is fully compatible with traditional Christianity, Islam and Judaism, but Pantheism is not.

So why does this philosophical discussion have any meaning for a too-busy person's consideration? We live in a universe that is "charged with the grandeur of God," according to Gerard Manley Hopkins. As we drive to work, take a walk in the park, teach our children to fish, ski down a mountain, we can "tip our hats" in acknowledgement of the Creator of all that exists in this amazing world.

Yet most of the time we simply take Nature and even our own beating hearts for granted. We live, move, have our being, walk through our days, sometimes with no recognition of the obvious, that each of us is a miracle. All living beings are miracles. Waking up each day is a miracle, in a real sense.

The obvious, as well as the infinite, is symbolized for us every day. Our keys are not in their usual place in our purses; we look all over the house; we return to the obvious place, our purses, and voila, they are zipped into the opposite side. We shop with our spouses all day for a new car, having first read *Consumer Report,* and find a car we really like at the first place we look. But, just in case, we go to five other dealers, only to return to the first selection, an obvious fit for us. As we prepare a rushed dinner, we run out of an ingredient and feel harassed until we remember an obvious substitute. We are given a pink slip at work and have to seek another job; looking back, we realize that the second job was an obvious fit for our talents.

When we review our lives, all our obvious choices and also those realities that break into our days, our apparent failures, our surprises and successes, our dreams and struggles, we realize that they are all pointing to Something or Someone

Infinite. We seek the Infinite, as we walk the paths of the obvious.

After a time, we begin to live more consciously, with an Awareness stance toward much that happens in our lives, and much that we ourselves make happen. And this spirit of Awareness leads us to act with Lovingkindness and Justice toward all that exists. The ancient Hebrew psalmist wrote: When I look at the heavens, the moon and the stars and see all You have created, who am I that you care so deeply for me? *(Psalm 8:3-4)*

CHAPTER 11:
KNOWING ALL MEN AND WOMEN
ARE CREATED EQUAL…BUT???

Little wonder that I have been called a "workaholic," not unlike many women in past decades. As a child of 3½ I looked after my brother, holding his bottle as I knelt on a chair by his buggy and one afternoon alerted my mother that his swing was beginning to come loose from the door jam. At 7 I was teaching the neighborhood doctor's third grade son to read and the physically handicapped girl named Ruthie how to skate. In the neighborhood I was the super-responsible kid that some way persuaded all of us not to burn down the abandoned house or do harm to other persons, animals, or properties. From ages 8 until 13 I babysat, and picked berries, beans and nuts, to buy my school books and clothes, and then later worked in the cannery and at theatres through my high school years. During college days I worked out my expenses and board and room with families, at Tommy Luke and other florists, and at any small job I could find.

Professionally I have taught with both women and men in high schools, universities, seminaries, and graduate schools. Administrative assignments have kept me busy from 7 a.m. until 10 or 11 p.m. as novice director, faculty chair, what we then called "superior," Provincial Leader, and other posts. In addition, I have also served as a pricer for a catalog order warehouse and as a bill auditor for a medical insurance company.

I mention these work venues because, when I look back at my life as a woman in a "man's world," as they referred to it then, I now see that in each role for which I was responsible I did experience the inequalities and instances of harassment of females (and some males) that have become common topics of conversation with the "Me-too" movement. However, I had several advantages that many women did not: (1) I had a father who taught me to "run like a bat out of hell" while saying to myself "don't mess with me, brother, or you will be sorry" if I found myself in a dangerous place, a strategy that became essential on several occasions when I worked in Baltimore, (2) my father believed what I said, and acted quickly and wisely if I told him that I had been threatened or propositioned, (3) my three brothers taught me how to fight for myself, and (4) one's own integrity is the most important virtue as far as I am concerned, so I am not a very submissive or easily convinced lady.

Nevertheless, instead of spending much time on what happened in the past, I urge us to recall that it was a different age. What seemed clever or funny or "boys will be boys" in the past, is harassment and uncouth non-professional behavior. Presently, it seems to me that we in the USA have begun to grown up, become more mature and more sensitive to diversity: of age, culture, religion, economic status, and of course, gender. We have watched women run for president, witnessed women serving as corporate heads, become aware of older citizens winning Olympic medals, and have also had the experience of men healing our woundedness as nurses.

SPIRITUALITY OF RECOGNITION OF GIFTS

But, what has all this gibberish got to do with spirituality on the run? Men and women were, and are, created equal, of equal value and significance—in the image of God, that is, gifted with intelligence and free will. That needs to be assumed and then recognized, as we work side by side. It is of course true that some women and men have been blessed with superior talents in various facets of our shared endeavor: like the black women who did the math for the space programs, the men who designed the arms on spacecraft, the counselor who reads body signals well and catches potential suicides before they happen, the pastor who knows his or her congregation so well that their preaching hits the target almost every Sunday.

St. Thomas Aquinas said that humility is truth. Humility recognizes truth: the truth of my own and the talents and liabilities of other people. If humility is inherent in our spirituality, we know and recognize the gifts of other persons, women and men, as well as our own. Many if not most people have gifts superior to ours in some respect. So, our entire project or corporation is better because of the pooled gifts of each woman and man. It's possible then, because we too are the beneficiaries of their talents, to be interiorly proud of that person, humbly recognizing their special gifts, not jealous or envious of them.

We can look for the special gifts of ourselves and of other women and men, and then recognize them, first within our own observations of other people. We can then honestly acknowledge the importance of each person to the entirety of every human endeavor.

Spirituality of Affirmation of Giftedness

If a lived spirituality means we put into practice daily our values, convictions, beliefs, and spiritual practices, then we need to affirm from Monday through Friday these gifts of our women and men colleagues, friends, or family members. We can do so verbally, in written form, at group gatherings, or on anniversaries or special occasions. It seems to be common practice to do "roasts" instead of "toasts" at many events. This kind of celebration often leaves the person sick at heart and not heartened by the words of those whom she or he needs for support and the energy to do better because one is appreciated.

I have observed that the workplace or party sites are locations where many put-downs occur. If a woman is just plain more intelligent so that her ideas are picked up by superiors, some men and women colleagues have put down that "Broad" with comments about her sleeping with the boss. If a woman is artistic and creates an attractive place for the Christmas party, she is referred to as a "Miss Happy Homemaker," with the snide inference that she hasn't a brain in her head. If a man excels in graciously connecting people, he is accused of "buttering them up" for some ulterior motive.

Instead of undermining colleagues, friends, or family members a healthy spirituality might lead us to say something like "That was a really innovative contribution" after her presentation, Or "how great to leave our computers behind and step into a colorful festive environment. Thanks for all the time it took." Or "You have a super way of forming community here, Bill." Or "You really keep this family connected, Joe."

A sincere affirmation goes a long way toward moving a person to become even more creative. It is a win-win for us, for her or him, and for our corporation or family.

SPIRITUALITY OF CONNECTIONS

An interviewee on Face the Nation made the point that the greatest problem in America today is loneliness, that we yearn for connections. Our children are now scattered throughout the world, the close relationships that existed in small towns and local churches seem to have disappeared, the neighborhood kids playing baseball or other games until mothers called them in for dinner has been replaced with games on an individual's hand-held cell phone.

Yet human beings were created to be social beings. The need for connectedness is still built into us. We connect on Facebook, Twitter, and dating services on our computers. We have learned new ways to connect. Some are not as healthy or deeply satisfying as face-to-face encounters.

When we are together, we sometimes connect clumsily. For example, a little alcohol at the Mardi Gras or Christmas or New Year's Party parties seems to free the tongue and lengthen the arms. I have watched "the girls" huddle together, so that they do not have to experience the pats and hugs and off-color jokes that are meant to be funny or endearing. I have also heard from attractive men that a party can be a pretty unbearable evening of come-on's or malicious remarks, especially if it is his first office party and he came to create some relationships beyond the demands of the daily work setting.

Would it not be lovely if, instead of these behaviors, our spirituality of service and concern and connectedness routed us to the table where we could pick up some bon-bons or a tray of champagne glasses to carry to a group of women or a woman standing alone? What about a firm handshake and some "let's get to know a little bit about each other's interests or job demands" talk with the new male employee? Maybe there could be some mutual help offered, again for the good of everybody working for the company.

SPIRITUALITY OF EMPATHY

Bad things happen to good people. Sometimes a female (or male) colleague loses a spouse, mother, father, child, or sibling. A sound spirituality does not say, "Oh, he/she is in a better place; don't worry." Or worse, the cruel "You are quite the number. You'll find somebody else soon." A gentle smile, sympathy note, small symbol, a cup of coffee, replacement or help on a project, proposal to serve at the funeral gathering, or some meaningful offer of oneself to the one grieving goes a long way. Trite spiritual expressions or rude or cruel comments do not express one's empathy very well, and may be very hurtful.

I am told that grief at the loss of a loved one takes about two years to heal. Also, many of us have found that little things we encounter daily remind us of the loved ones. A spirituality of empathy allows TIME to the grieving one, who may be a little sad, edgy, distracted, inefficient for a while. It is important that he or she shows up to be with other people, does the best work possible, and keeps involved in their supportive relationships with us.

***

The workplace, where we spend many hours, is kind of a "cubicle cathedral," in a way. There are vast opportunities for recognition of Wisdom, affirmation of Goodness, and empathy for the Beauty of relationships. The same is true within our family or friendship circles. Much of my life I have spent reflecting on the Infinite Wisdom, Goodness, and Beauty of God. For me, and possibly for many, the workplace can be a microcosm of that Great Reality.

CHAPTER 12:
TAMING THE VIOLENCE WITHIN US

For years I was puzzled and touched deeply by the movie, *The Burning Bed*, where Francine Hughes (Farrah Fawcett) suffers the abuse of her husband, Mickey (Paul Le Mat), for almost a decade because she cannot find any help. When a drunken Mickey rapes her and then passes out, Francine pours gasoline over him and lights him on fire. In the ensuing blaze, Mickey dies as the house goes up in flames. Francine leaves the scene with her children. For years, my brother was employed as a steam engineer for a women's prison in Purdy, Washington; and some of those women had also taken drastic measures to rid themselves and their children of violent spouses, and were serving prison terms as murderers.

But the movie and my brother's stories led me to ask myself about the violence within me and all of us, and where it fits with a spirituality of love and concern for the all People of God as well as the earth they inhabit. I realized that I would be a very vicious wolf woman if someone raped or harmed my children deliberately. Or, perhaps any children if I found myself in the arena where this was happening to them!

OUR COMPETITIVE SOCIETY

"Me first."

"America first."

"My family or my church or my neighborhood or my culture is best."

Violence softened somewhat to an overall competitive consciousness.

We may even have watched, on a snowy day, the driver who had to pass all of us to get ahead on the freeway, only to skid into the ditch ahead. We learn the language of competition and win/lose from Little League days until we struggle with self-identity at the time of retirement when we wonder if we are no longer productive winners but worthless losers to society. And all of us watch daily our two camps, Democrats and Republicans, fight for a win/lose stance, and not necessarily for the win/win common good of most or all Americans.

When I was a young child, my Mom made many loaves of bread to share with neighborhood families, a neighbor shared apples and homemade vinegar from that same tree, people traded ration coupons, and folks helped each other with building projects. World War II had started, but people on the home front acted collaboratively, not competitively, trying together to do all they could for a common effort, the "war effort."

In this decade, however, competition has made it possible for some people to become "winners" and many others "losers." Though statistics vary from year to year, and are dependent on the one reporting, a recent figure was this: the richest **1 percent** in the United States now own more additional income than the bottom **90 percent**.

This makes me wonder if our tendency toward violence and a more nuanced competitive consciousness have been shaping us into competitors on all fronts. Instead of the win/win we witnessed formerly, we seem to be leaning toward win/lose in precious and significant portions of our lives: family life, church life, political, and economic life. Looking through the lens of win/lose directs us to blame-games, not compassion and neighborly sharing or "reaching across the aisle" or making a global difference for the lives of humankind.

THE WARREN BUFFETT, BILL GATES WAY

Certainly, competition is not bad in itself. We compete with ourselves to earn higher grades, to improve our golf games, to prepare for a job that fits our innate talents, to become healthier physically, and to be more loving and compassionate. We engage in healthy competition with other companies, challenging each other to produce better products. Competing with ourselves to form a more efficient company can make it possible for us to enrich the lives of other people who do not have the education or health or opportunities that we have had.

During this last decade I have become an admirer of two men who not only competed to build better companies but also to serve more people with the earnings they produced. Warren Buffett in 2006 made the announcement that he would be giving his entire fortune away to charity, committing 85 percent of it to the Bill and Melinda Gates Foundation. Not only did he give during his life billions in personal donations to the needy, but he also challenged his wealthy colleagues to share half of their resources with those who were not so well-endowed. The Bill and Melinda Gates Foundation, inspired by David Rockefeller, decided to spend their assets on global issues which were apparently ignored by governments, investing in the empowerment of people through education, conquest of diseases that have almost wiped out total populations, and on environmental issues that could also wipe out the health of the planet. Bill and Melinda have built an organization that aims to get resources to the poorest people in the world—and in ways that are sustainable for the future. Not bad for two boys from Omaha, Nebraska and Seattle, Washington.

It is quite possible to change the 1%-90% statistical pattern. One of Islam's spiritual norms is that one gives yearly 2.5% of available income to care for the poor and disadvantaged. If each of us adopted that practice, alone the statistics of poverty in America would be altered.

CHANNELING THE ENERGIES
OF VIOLENCE AND COMPETITIVENESS

A spirituality that moves us toward the use of our gifts for the betterment of those in that poorest 90 percent category, which empowers them to sharpen their talents through education, which improves global issues for people and Mother Earth—these are healthy and loving ways to channel the energies within us that can explode into violence or unhampered greedy competition. This kind of channeling resources is a genuine harmonization of spirituality and purposeful investment of our time, treasure, and talents. Not only that, we then have the resources to engage other people in meaningful productive works that utilize their gifts and insure a sustainable future for themselves, their children, and that part of the world they inhabit, truly a win/win for all.

Years ago I read about saints who could have used their powers to become either great saints or great sinners. I have come to believe that it is true. We can channel energies, as we have done in making hydrogen bombs which created unimaginable forces of violence and destruction. Or, we can capture the amazing energies from the sun to power entire cities.

***

Taming the violence that resides within all of us can create powers for Good that humanity has never yet dreamed of.

CHAPTER 13:
FINDING SPIRITUALITY AMIDST
THE SECULAR QUEST

One glance at any headline, storefront, billboard along the freeway, or television commercial and any visitor can guess that he or she has landed in a secular USA. A few years ago, our newspaper told the story of a warehouse that had just burned to the ground, with the discovery of the charred corpse of a homeless man. The headline read something like "$250,00 Warehouse Fire." Only as an aside at the end of the article was there mention of the sad death of a homeless human being involved in that fire. I have heard or read stories of wars, floods, earthquakes, family and national and international disasters measured in dollars.

This is the world in which we live and love and work alongside our other secular sisters and brothers. Instead of condemning secularism, perhaps a rich spirituality can be discovered in the secular quest for what is Good, True, and Beautiful.

UNCOVERING THE GOOD

Step back in history to the Great Depression in the USA and walk forward to today. Almost everything we notice or think about as we move along this "sentimental journey" has been developed for the Good of humankind by human beings. Consider: sidewalks with slanted corners for wheelchair users, plastic chairs in front of the Bistro, cars that zip by, polyester/wool sweaters, nylon padded jackets, air-conditioned office buildings, jets that fly overhead, walkers for babies, rollators for seniors, neon signs—one could list 100 items in a very short time.

Advances in medicine have made it possible for people to live longer and with greater mobility, so we notice people from every generation walking or "scootering" alongside us, as well as those with handicaps. Many now fly to Europe or take cruises to Alaska. Formerly their health limits would have kept them forever inside their homes and separated from social and work life.

Computers and other technological advances have allowed us to be in immediate contact with citizens all over the world and to work together on multiple projects and scientific advances. At one time we would have waited for a month to receive the results from Japan or Germany or Australia of experiments being done on a joint project.

Food preservation, and shipping of fresh citrus fruits have eliminated diseases like scurvy. Vaccinations have almost eradicated diseases like small pox. Furniture is designed for bad backs.

The output figures on automobiles put together every single day are mind-boggling. With the utilization of robots, the numbers have become staggering. Freeways and traffic patterns have not been able to accelerate fast enough to prevent the snarls that have resulted.

Our gifted ingenious human brains have allowed us to look at needs around us and to design or invent something Good to take care of almost every need. When we feel like moaning about the evils in our world today, ten minutes listing the Good things is really salutary.

EXAMINING THE TRUE

Instant replay allows us to decide results during athletic events to the fraction of a second. Fact-checking on speeches by presidents and other public figures can readily disclose "fake news." Though we are tempted to consider the oft-repeated message as True, it is wise to examine what is advertised or what is held to be an enduring Truth.

There are deeper and richer Truths that abide through the centuries, to which we appeal for their longevity and the ways they have enriched human lives. In the Jain religion, in addition to the principle of non-violence, one embraces non-attachment to material things and non-attachment to one's own ideas and Truths, recognizing that Truth has many faces among the peoples of the world. Thus, we let go of "my way or the highway" attitudes, frozen positions that have led to more than one divorce or war.

An advantage of sending our children to liberal arts colleges is that they learn to think and write critically, to do their research and back up their positions instead of considering their opinions as absolute Truth. Also, the professional journals we ourselves read, that have been juried to lay out tested factual information, help us grow and speak with conviction to our colleagues.

STANDING IN WONDER BEFORE THE BEAUTIFUL

Aleksandr Solzhenitsyn wrote: "Beauty will save the world." Our world of today so needs Transformation, Hope, and BEAUTY. He says:

> Writers and artists have a great opportunity: to conquer the lie! In battle with the lie, art has always been victorious, always wins out, visibly, incontrovertibly for all! The lie can stand up and win out over much in the world—but not over art. And as soon as the lie is dispersed, the repulsive nakedness of violence is exposed, and violence will collapse in impotence.

Even under adverse circumstances human beings create art. Japanese in the American internment camps created incredible wooden carvings and pottery from local clay. There are records of imprisoned German Jews forming classical choral groups, knowing that their lives could end the next day. Many of us have seen dolls, replicas of dolls, and other art forms made by

Black slaves in the South. Beauty was indeed salvific for them, raised their spirits, and added joy to their lives.

People of every nation have learned that Beauty endures, so we have built magnificent museums in the USA and throughout the world. In fact, it breaks our hearts when they are bombed to extinction, because 4,000 years of recorded human history was lost with the shattering of an ancient statue.

We may forget much of what we have read or thought. But we remember, especially when we are feeling sad, the beautiful double rainbow, the dew on the spider web, the waves of the ocean, the smile of a child, the lines on grandmother's face. People love to live near lakes, mountains, and redwood trees. When we travel, most people choose places that are extraordinarily beautiful: like Hawaii, Alaska, the Bahamas.

We stand in awe as waves crash against the rocks, rising hundreds of feet in the air at times. It is truly a spiritual experience to stand in wonder before Beauty. Matthew Fox, noticing that residents in an area of New York kept themselves inside, drawing down their shades, exhibiting a dark spirit and a dark environment. The world changed for many of them when he taught them to make rubbings of manhole covers and objects right in their neighborhood. Beauty is all around us.

***

As long as we are alive we can look around us for the Good, the True, and the Beautiful. People will tell me that they find God among the trees when they walk in the forest, or in the words of a poet, or in the goodness of persons who went out of their way for them. This is indeed living spirituality in our secular world.

CHAPTER 14:
PAYING ATTENTION TO DESIRES

St. Ignatius of Loyola, Founder of the Society of Jesus, in his writings about the spiritual life, emphasized the importance of listening to our desires, our deepest desires. Mark Thibodeux. SJ, Novice Master and author of *God's Voice Within,* explains this surprise feature of spirituality very well:

> Probably the most surprising feature of the Ignatian approach [to spirituality] is the premise that God's will can often be discovered in our "great desires." Much of Christian spirituality presumes that our desires are bad and will lead us to sinful actions. Ignatius believed that our problem was not desiring too much but rather desiring too little. He believed that we sin not because we've followed our desires but because our desires are "disordered." That is, the whole collection of our desires is placed in the wrong order, leaving us to follow petty, superficial desires rather than the great big desires that God has placed in our hearts. What are these "great desires?" Ultimately, they are variations of actions that will lead to faith, hope and love for God and our fellow neighbor.

Allow me to offer a few examples. Not long ago I was speaking to a person who has been working in the technological field for about 20 years. The person has an MA in Pastoral Theology and a great desire to do work in spirituality, to spend time with people, even to walk with patients on their last journey in hospice programs. Yet, like countless others in the USA and elsewhere, the security of a large salary, of working in a defined field, of avoiding the necessity of taking the initiative to seek out or to design a niche that fits one's personality and gifts are too persuasive to motivate him to change to a call he deeply desires to follow. We may know friends who tell us of their deepest desires to end some relationships, to pursue a degree, to give themselves time to take up music or art, or undertake risks that would enrich them as human persons, while empowering them to offer their richness to other human beings. However, motivating themselves to take the first steps toward realizing their "great desires" seems to be beyond them.

The major challenge of this book is that of balancing our spiritual and active lives in our chaotic world. Each year human inventions set before us more and more attractive choices. To determine which ones we deeply desire, and which ones fit our personalities, and which ones would offer most to other human beings, takes careful and prayerful discernment.

IDENTIFYING THE DESIRES OF ONE'S HEART

Human choices are often beyond the merely rational or reasonable. "The heart has its reasons of which the mind knows nothing," Pascal said.

What if we could give ourselves permission to dream and let our hearts ask, "What if I could (do, be, live) what I most desire?" Sometimes we "list-makers" can identify and jot down these desires. Then we can imagine ourselves in those settings to discover if they leave us with a "yuk" or "yum" feeling, as my niece used to describe these leanings. St. Ignatius also wrote about contemplating a scene from Scripture or another reality through imagination.

Thus, imagining ourselves in a setting helps us realize whether the desire is a really deep desire or a superficial one that probably would not be comfortable for very long. That makes it easier to prioritize and possibly hit one that seems really on the mark for us.

Realistically Looking at Desires
That Fit One's Personality and Gifts

Obviously at 5'2" I would never make a basketball team, and having been changed from a leftie to one who writes with my right hand and has little hand-eye coordination, any athletic desires would go to the bottom of the list. Examination of our successes and where we felt most at-home with ourselves is a good place to start when we try to identify which desires fit best. Friends who know us well, spouses, supervisors, colleagues, spiritual counselors or directors, children, and those whom we have served are often helpful in letting us know how we have touched their lives at the deepest levels.

I spent most of my high school days sitting with other students, helping them with math or science or literature. Teachers and friends predicted that I would be a professor some day; but I insisted I would be a medical doctor. As years have passed, I the professor realize that I do not like to hear about "organ recitals" at table conversations or any other time or place; perhaps I would not have lasted very long as a medical doctor. Sometimes we need others to help us see ourselves and how we could best serve other people.

Surveying What the World Needs Now

As the song goes, "What the world needs now is love, sweet love..."

WHAT THE WORLD NEEDS NOW
by Jackie DeShannon

What the world needs now is love, sweet love
It's the only thing that there's just too little of
What the world needs now is love, sweet love,
No not just for some, but for everyone.

Lord, we don't need another mountain,
There are mountains and hillsides enough to climb
There are oceans and rivers enough to cross,
Enough to last till the end of time.

Each of us expresses love for that world in a different way. So, we need to be match-makers for ourselves: matching our desires, our gifts and skills, and the needs of people around us. At this time in history, that task is nothing short of overwhelming. There are spiritual, cultural, economic, political, social, familial, corporate, environmental needs, with thousands of needs under each domain. Nevertheless, we can narrow our responses. In a recent conversation with someone, she and I were able to focus on a major financial issue by considering her deepest desire, the place where her heart is most profoundly touched and which has the best chance of making a difference to people in the future.

**

For us Americans, examining our deepest desires sounds a bit wu-wu. We have become accustomed to looking at concrete data, dollars and cents, income and expenses, goals and objectives, and so forth. To listen to the language of the heart is not as familiar. But, listening to the desires of the heart, motivating ourselves to take the first steps toward realizing them, and figuring out ways that we can thus humanize our world in unique ways, could have the pay-off of a very rewarding life.

CHAPTER 15:
MYSTICS CAN TALK TO EACH OTHER

One of the phenomena that baffles me today is the reluctance of people to talk to each other, as in:

"I do not talk to my mother anymore."

"My brother and I are not on speaking terms."

"My sister and I cut the ties a long time ago."

On the other hand, there are those who seem to wish to speak to everyone, often in a very loud voice, or to reveal on Facebook personal information that most people would reserve for a confessional or psychiatrist's office. I recall my discomfort, standing for a long time in a DMV line listening to a cell phone user relay very private information for the ears of 40 people.

To begin, a few words about mystics and mysticism may be important for our reflections. Googling comes up with this: "Mysticism is a belief that union with or absorption into a deity or the Absolute, or the spiritual apprehension of knowledge inaccessible to the intellect, may be attained through contemplation and self-surrender." And Webster tells us that it is "the belief that direct knowledge of God, spiritual truth, or ultimate reality can be attained through subjective experience (such as intuition or insight)." I resonate with the thoughts of Karl Rahner: "When man [sic] is with God in awe and love, then he is praying. In the days ahead, we must become mystics (one who experiences God for real) or be nothing at all." Is the absence of these experiences of awe, of letting the other be other, the reason some people have no grounds for speaking to each other? Do they expect the other to be a clone of themselves, instead of each person existing as a unique mysterious creation?

Mystics can speak to each other, hear each other, understand to an extent the experiences of the other. They do not argue belief systems, nor theology, nor doctrines, nor right and wrong. They do not expect win/lose conclusions. They do not strive toward one answer to their questioning. They speak of the awe and wonder of their personal experiences. The friendship between the Buddhist Dalai Lama and the Trappist Monk Thomas Merton is by now legendary. Merton died at the Monastery of the Dalai Lama where they had been sharing spiritual experiences. Mystics come in many colors and faces and religions.

YOUR PERSONAL EXPERIENCES
OF INSCRUTABLE HAPPENINGS

Lest we sound wu-wu, perhaps we can recall times in our lives when we were simply embraced by a sense of awe and wonder, not aware of ourselves, simply taken up with the beauty or goodness or amazing truth of that which we just experienced, quite unable to describe with precision the inscrutable happening that had just enveloped our being. Think of a few:

- Maybe it was the first time you gazed on your new baby, a life you helped create,

- Or watched the dance of the Northern Lights as you sat on the lakeshore,

- Or were struck by the beauty of a person's character or wisdom,

- Or were moved to tears by the words or poetry or literature someone uttered,

- Or soared with your whole being as a musical score was being presented,

- Or heard a message that completely shifted your perspective on a theological or scientific or economic position,

- Or felt embraced and one-with that which is infinite,
  Sacred, Mysterious, totally Other.

It is that sense of being mystically caught up in a Reality
other than oneself that we have in common with the Mystics.

WONDER AT THE MYSTERY OF THE HUMAN PERSON

It is a delightful moment when we watch a child discover his
toes. We ourselves are full of wonder at the ways our body
systems work together to keep us alive: our heart keeps beating,
our lungs keep taking in air, our ears pick up the sounds of the
oncoming train, our legs can run marathons in emergencies.

And how is it that we can solve problems or find substitute
resolutions when one answer does not work? Or create vehicles,
robots, drones, computers, and iPhones? When we review
history, we realize that humankind's gifts of intelligence and
free will have invented unbelievable creations. Listening to
programs about Nobel prize or Pulitzer prize winners leaves us
with a deep sense of awe and gratitude.

This sense lifts our hearts too when we hear Bernstein's
music, Shakespeare's dramas, Hopkins' or Mary Oliver's poetry,
and the new work, Hamilton. From where does such creativity
and originality come?

INSCRUTABLE UNFOLDING
OF MOTHER NATURE'S GIFTS

Oregonians love the lakes, rivers, ocean, fir trees, birds,
deer, and all the wonders of Mother Nature available to them
every day. We can lift our faces to the rain and know that new
life will be nourished by the showers that ruin a new crepe
dress or a poster we just painted.

Those who embrace an environmental spirituality hold a
deep reverence for our Common Home, and express their beliefs
in their tender care of all of nature, of the entire biosphere.
They are the ones who ride bikes to keep the air from absorbing
gas fumes. They eat vegetarian food, because animals need to

consume so much vegetation and live on large sections of land. We learn from their mystical sense of appreciation for all creation.

AWE AT THE COSMOS

Perhaps you too spent much time lying on your back, making figures from clouds, or studying the stars, or feeling amazed at the Milky Way, or wondering about Heaven "up there" some place. Scientific discoveries have broadened and deepened our awareness of the ever-expanding Universe. The Cosmos is always beyond any reality our hearts and minds can ever dream. But our reflections on it can certainly diminish the weight of our problems.

In future decades we will learn more and more about our solar system and the heavens. We may even travel in the space about which we dreamed. As John's Gospel sys: "God is always greater than our hearts."

***

Recognizing the Mysterious in each other, viewing the mysterious in our own experiences, in all human beings, in the world around us, and beyond us in the entire Cosmos broadens our perspective on everything that exists. It allows into our lives many kinds of "other," all of which can enrich our own lives. Looking at all of creation with the wonder of a Mystic will keep us sharing our personal experiences, growing deeper—and talking to each other.

ABOUT THE AUTHOR

PERSONAL INFORMATION

Dr. Cecilia Ranger's lifelong commitment is that of educating and drawing out of people questions which will lead them to personal integration, finding a meaningful life path, discovering a spiritual home, and determining a vocation in life—thus, her commitment to education, philosophy, theology, facilitating retreats, and serving as spiritual director. Her passion is dialogue among the religious traditions, to bring together diverse positions on spirituality and ethics—in life situations, conversations, and in the workplace—as a means of helping to bring about world peace. So, it's been a rich life of interactions with God, people, and the beautiful world—all of which have taught her much about the rhythm of action and contemplation, two faces of the same love.

MINISTERIAL INFORMATION

- Former Mt. Angel Seminary Professor & Spiritual Director;
- Spiritual Director & Professor, St. Mary's Seminary and University, Baltimore, MD;
- President of Oregon Sisters of the Holy Names;
- Chair/Dean of Religion & Philosophy at Marylhurst University;
- Board of Trustees Member, Marylhurst University;
- Adjunct Professor at Marylhurst University, San Francisco Theological Seminary, Clark Community College, George Fox University;
- Pastoral Assistant at the Madeleine Church, Portland, Oregon;
- Facilitator of Workshops on Spiritual Life, Theology, or Scripture;
- Consultant for Leadership Groups; Co-Minister at Marylhurst University;
- Spiritual & Retreat Director for persons of many Faith traditions.

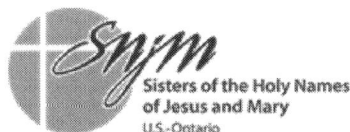

Sisters of the Holy Names
of Jesus and Mary
U.S.-Ontario

Dr. Cecilia A. Ranger, SNJM

YOU MAY WISH TO READ

Augustine, Saint. *City of God*

Barron, Robert Emmet. *Seeds of the Word: Finding God in the Culture*

Bold, Robert. *Man for All Seasons*

Bourgeault, Cynthia. *The Heart of Centering Prayer: Nondual Christianity in Theory and Practice*

Grof, Christina and Stanislav. *Spiritual Emergency: When Personal Transformation Becomes a Crisis*

Hoffman, Dominic. *The Life Within: The Prayer of Union*

Hopkins, Gerard Manley. *Poems and Prose* (Penguin Classics)

John of the Cross. *Dark Night of the Soul*

Johnson. Elizabeth A. *Ask the Beasts: Darwin and the God of Love*

May, Gerald. *Care of Mind, Care of Spirit*

Monroe, James. *"The Adolescent Brain in Meditation,"* citing Sara Lazar and her team at Harvard Medical School

Northwest Bishops (USA and Canada). *Pastoral Letter, The Columbia River Watershed: Caring for Creation and the Common Good*

Pope Frances. *Laudato Si*

Rossi, Holly Lebowitz. *Seven CEOs with Devout Religious Beliefs* (Fortune 11/11/2014)

Rumi, Jalal ad-Din Muhammad. *The Essential Rumi*

Vipassana Meditation Rehabilitation and Research Trust for North American Correctional Facilities in the United States.

Zylowska, Lidia MD. *The Mindfulness Prescription for Adult ADHD*

57203332R00052

Made in the USA
Columbia, SC
07 May 2019